Reading Start

Kristy Stevens

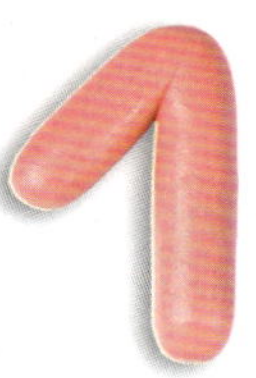

WorldCom ELT

How to Read Reading Start

Illustration

Illustrations designed to help predict the story while reading

Get Ready

Pre-reading questions designed to help students broaden their background knowledge and increase their interest in the topic of the unit

Passage

Informative and high-interest fiction / nonfiction story that develops students' reading skill and expands knowledge

Key Words

Vocabulary activities with photographs designed to practice key words in the story

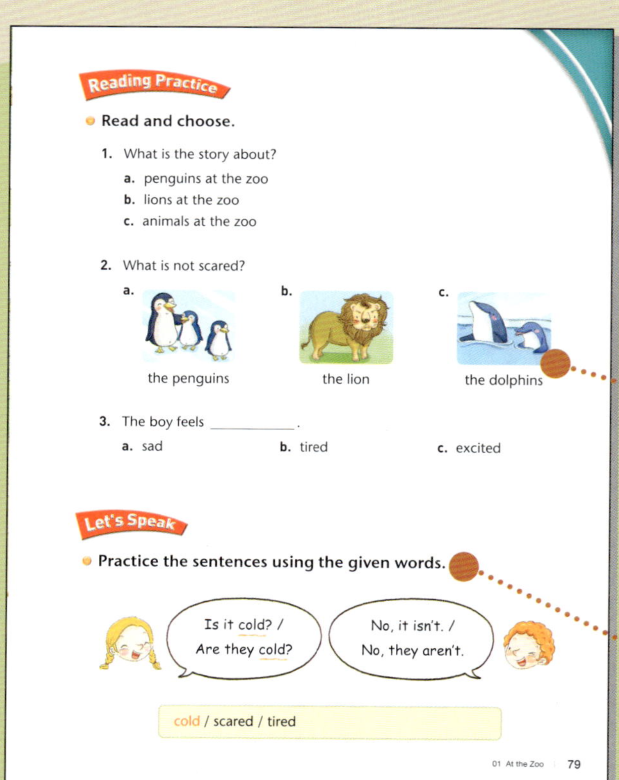

Reading Practice

Comprehension questions designed to test students' understanding of the passage and develop key reading skills such as the main idea and details

Let's Speak

Speaking practice to improve students' ability to express the key structure from the unit

Word Practice

Variations in vocabulary activities to reinforce the key words from the unit

Listening Practice

Listening exercises to improve students' ability to understand key words or key structure

Activity

Grammar exercises to improve students' ability to understand key grammar point

Do It

Activities related to the reading content that can be used for extended speaking and writing practice and offer in-depth studies of the unit

Contents

01 My Monster Family

 T01/04

Boo! My **name** is Spook.

I am a ghost.

Say hello to my **dad**.

He is a zombie.

Say hello to my **mom**.

She is a witch.

Say hello to my **brother** and **sister**.

They are vampires.

We are a monster **family**.

Get Ready

How many family members do you have?

Key Words

● **Listen and point.** T02

| mom | brother | name | dad | sister | family |

Read and choose.

1. What is the story about?

   a. a ghost family   **b.** a vampire family   **c.** a monster family

2. What is Spook?

   a. 
   a ghost

   b. 
   a zombie

   c. 
   a witch

3. How many are in Spook's family?

   a. 3   **b.** 4   **c.** 5

Let's Speak

Practice the sentences using the given words.

❶ He / She

❷ ghost / zombie / witch / vampire

🟠 **Look, choose and write.**

1. 

2. 

3. 

name   dad   mom   brother   sister   family

4. 

5. 

6. 

🟠 **Listen and choose.**  T03

O X

O X

O X

Look, read and circle.

1. 

I | is / am | a ghost.

2. 

He | is / are | a zombie.

3. 

They | am / are | vampires.

Do It

Look at the picture and complete the sentences.

1. I ___am___ David.　　2. She _______ Jane.

3. He _______ Rick.　　4. They _______ Spot and Fluffy.

A Royal Family

T05/08

Who is he?

He is my father, King Butter.

Who is she?

She is my mother, Queen Toast.

Who are they?

They are my brothers, Prince Knife and Prince Fork.

Who are you?

I am Princess Jam.

Together, we live in Sandwich Land.

Get Ready

How many family members are there in the picture?

Key Words

Listen and point. T06

prince

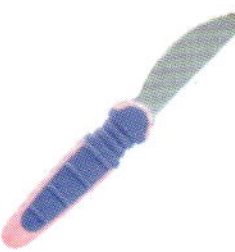

knife

butter

queen

princess

king

Read and choose.

1. What is the story about?

    a. a great family   **b.** a hungry family   **c.** a royal family

2. What is 'I'?

    a.    **b.**    **c.** 

    Queen Toast   Prince Fork   Princess Jam

3. They live in _____________ Land.

    a. Pizza   **b.** Sandwich   **c.** Hamburger

Let's Speak

Practice the sentences using the given words.

❶ he / she

❷ father / mother / brother / sister

- **Look and match.**

1. 

2. 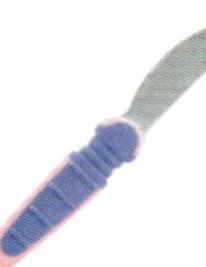

king
butter
queen
knife
prince
princess

3. 

4. 

5. 

6. 

Listening Practice

- **Listen and choose.**  T07

1  O X

2  O X

3  O X

● **Look, read and choose.**

1. 

I
He

   is King Butter.

2. 

He
She

   is Queen Toast.

3.

He
They

   are Prince Knife and Prince Fork.

Do It

● **Match and say.**

UNIT 2

01

My Robot, Turbo!

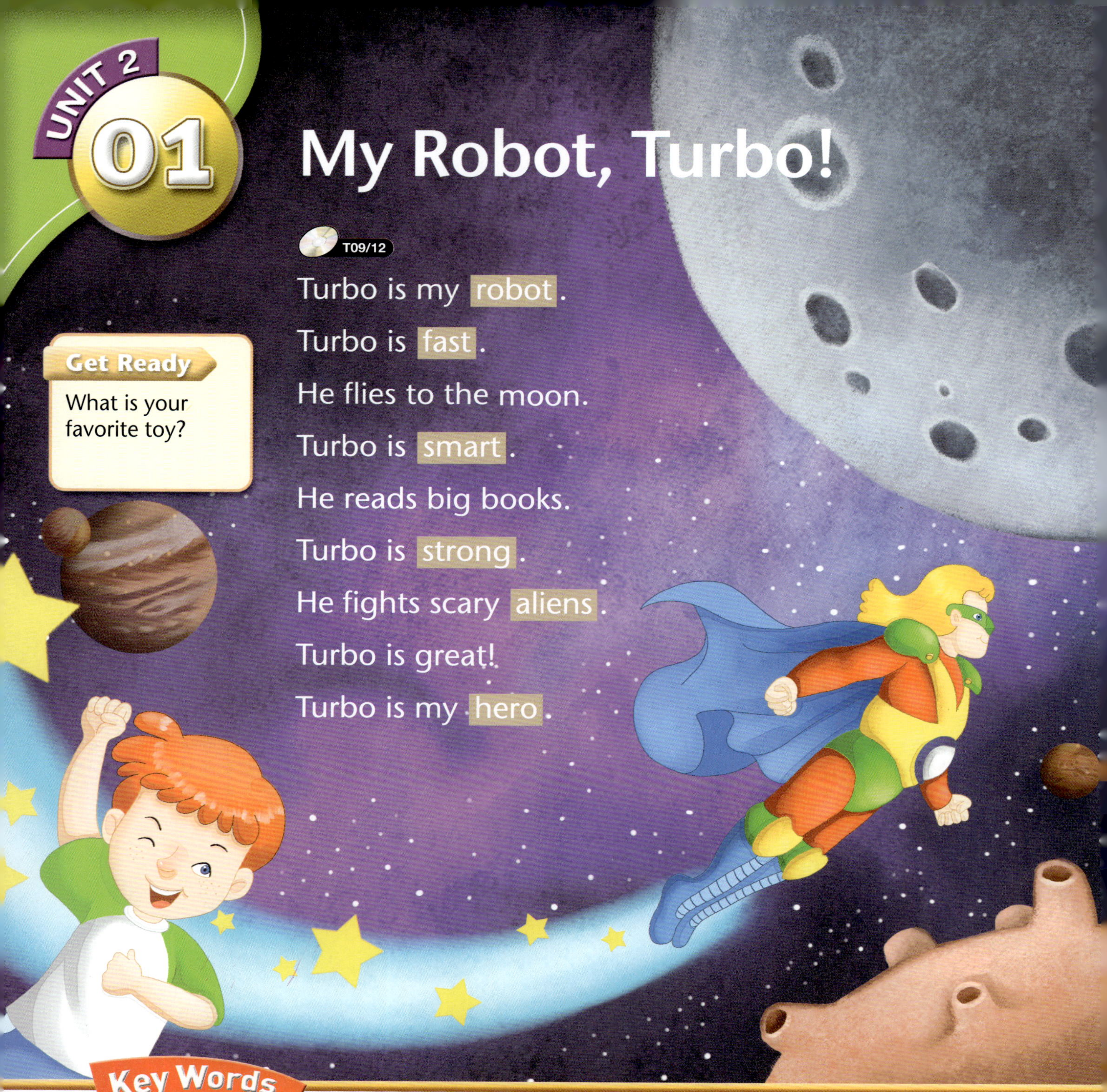

T09/12

Turbo is my robot.

Turbo is fast.

He flies to the moon.

Turbo is smart.

He reads big books.

Turbo is strong.

He fights scary aliens.

Turbo is great!

Turbo is my hero.

Get Ready

What is your favorite toy?

Key Words

Listen and point. T10

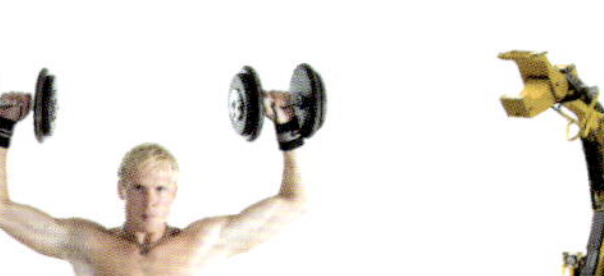

strong

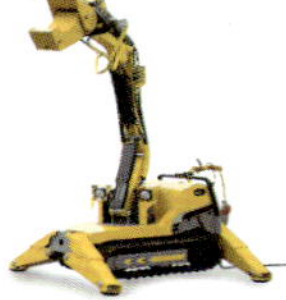

robot

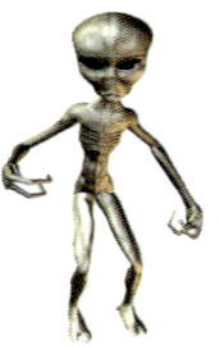

alien

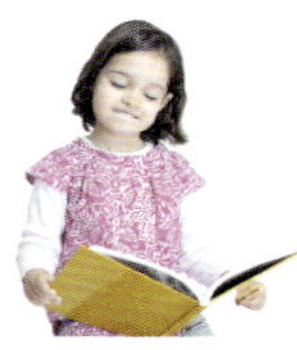

smart

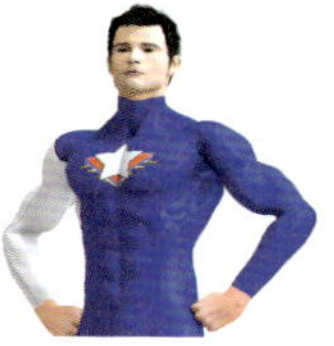

hero

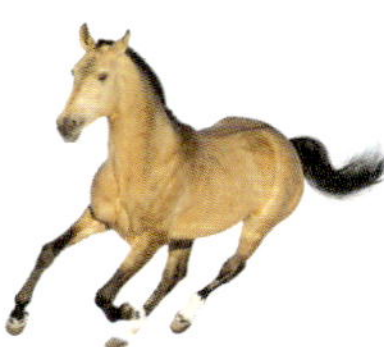

fast

● Read and choose.

1. What is the story about?

    a. my pet   **b.** my robot   **c.** my alien

2. What does Turbo do?

    a. 

    bakes cookies

    b. 

    watches TV

    c. 

    reads big books

3. Turbo is my _____________.

    a. family   **b.** neighbor   **c.** hero

Let's Speak

● Practice the sentences using the given words.

fast / smart / strong / great

🔸 **Look, unscramble and write.**

1. 

____

rheo

2. 

____

tafs

3. 

____

borto

4. 

____

enali

5. 

____

mstar

6. 

____

stngro

Listening Practice

🔸 **Listen and choose.**  T11

O | X

O | X

O | X

Activity

Look, read and circle.

1. 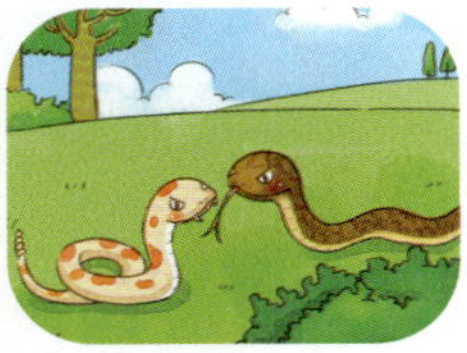

They are fast / scary .

2. 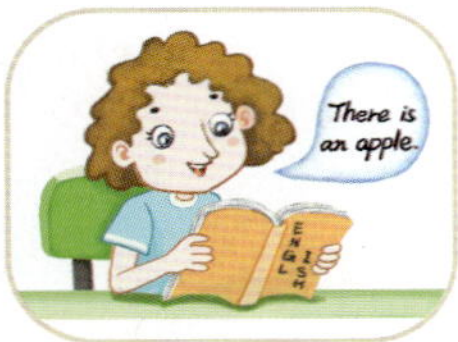

She is big / smart .

3. 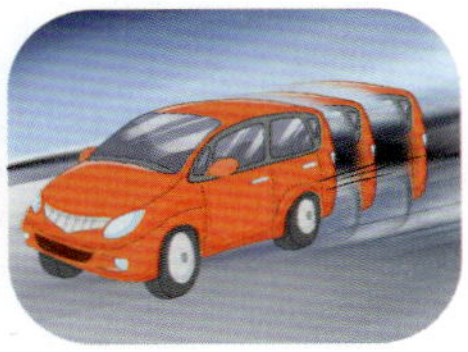

It is fast / strong .

Do It

Look, choose and sort.

Fast	Scary	Smart	Strong

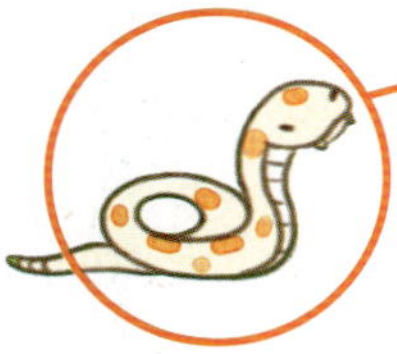
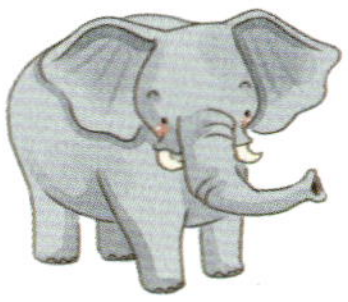
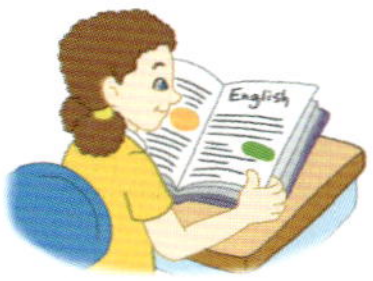

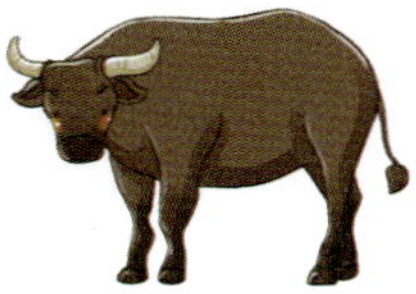
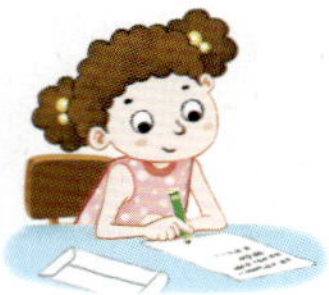
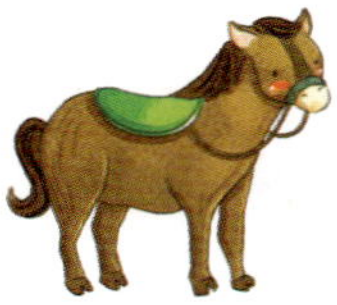
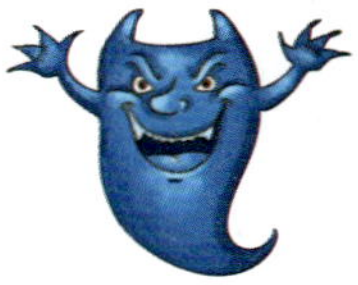
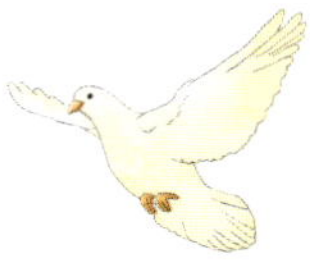

UNIT 2

02

My Fun Stickers

T13/16

There are ten stickers in my sticker book.

There are sparkly stars.

There is a vanilla cupcake.

There are colorful racecars.

There is a fuzzy rabbit.

There are sharp pencils.

There is a pretty mermaid.

And I want ten more!

Get Ready

What kind of stickers do you like to have?

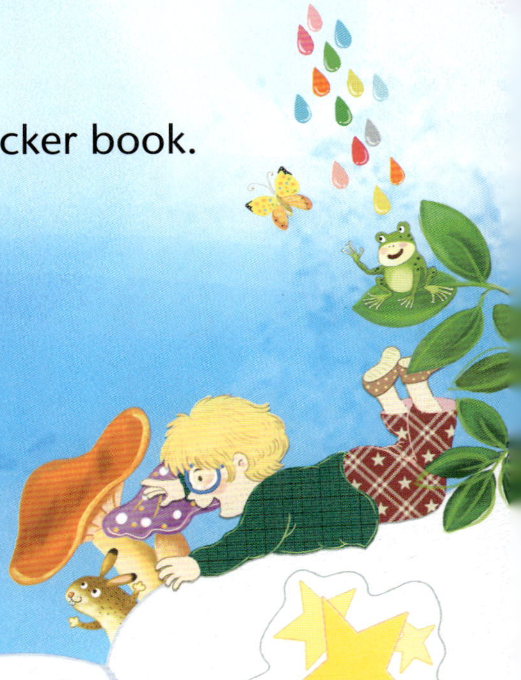

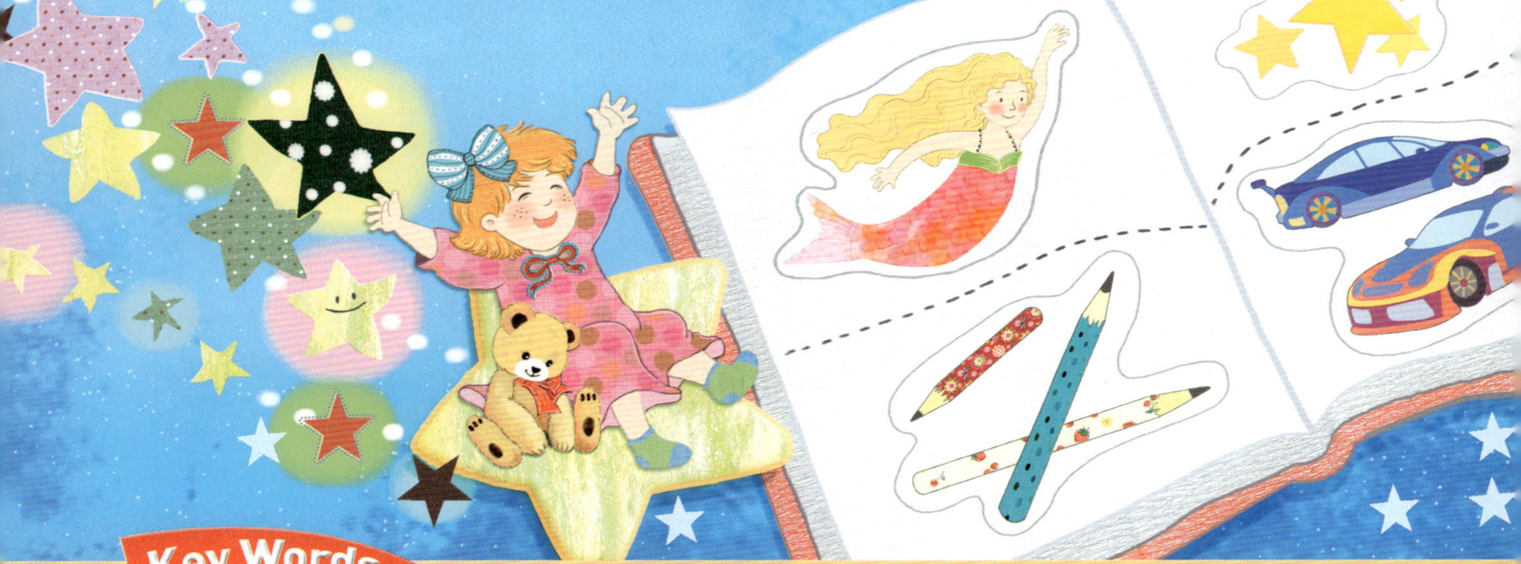

Key Words

- **Listen and point.** T14

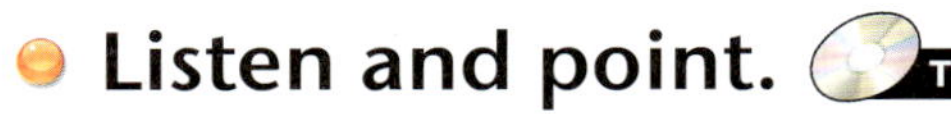

star

sticker

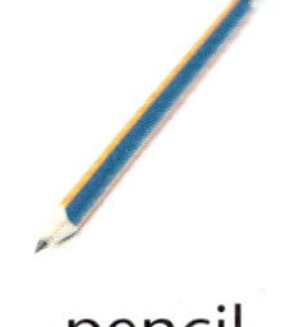

pencil

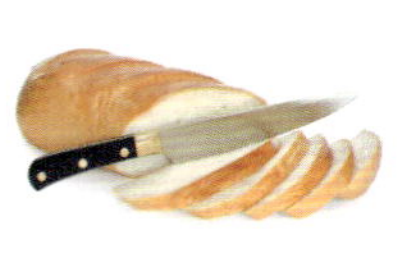

sharp

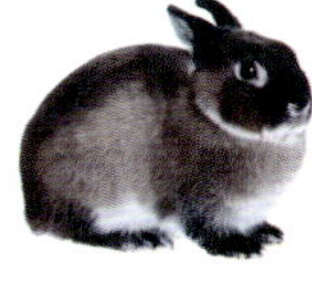

rabbit

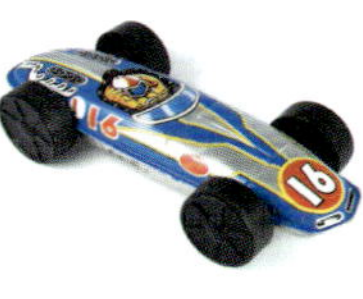

colorful

Read and choose.

1. What is the story about?

    a. cards   **b.** pictures   **c.** stickers

2. What are colorful?

    a. 

    stars

    b. 

    racecars

    c. 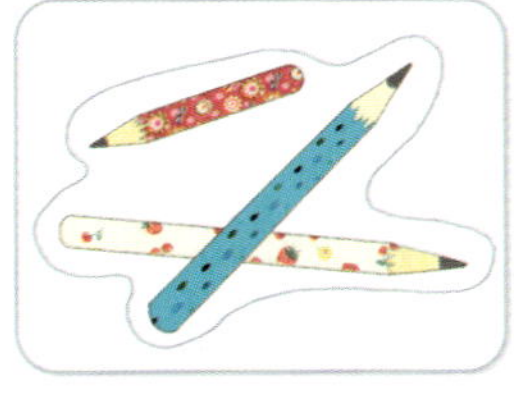

    pencils

3. There is not a ______________ in my sticker book.

    a. cupcake   **b.** flower   **c.** mermaid

Let's Speak

Practice the sentences using the given words.

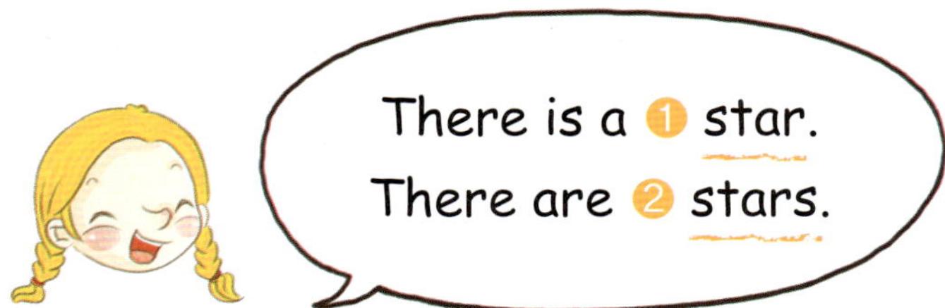

❶ star / cupcake / racecar / rabbit / pencil / mermaid

❷ stars / cupcakes / racecars / rabbits / pencils / mermaids

● **Look and complete.**

1. 

pen☐i☐

2. 

☐olor☐ul

3. 

☐a☐bit

4. 

sti☐☐er

5. 

st☐☐

6. 

☐☐arp

● **Listen and choose.** T15

1 

O X

2 

O X

3 

O X

Look, read and circle.

1.   There are   sharp / sparkly   stars.

2.   There are   fuzzy / colorful   racecars.

3.   There are   sharp / fuzzy   pencils.

Do It

Draw your items and talk about them.

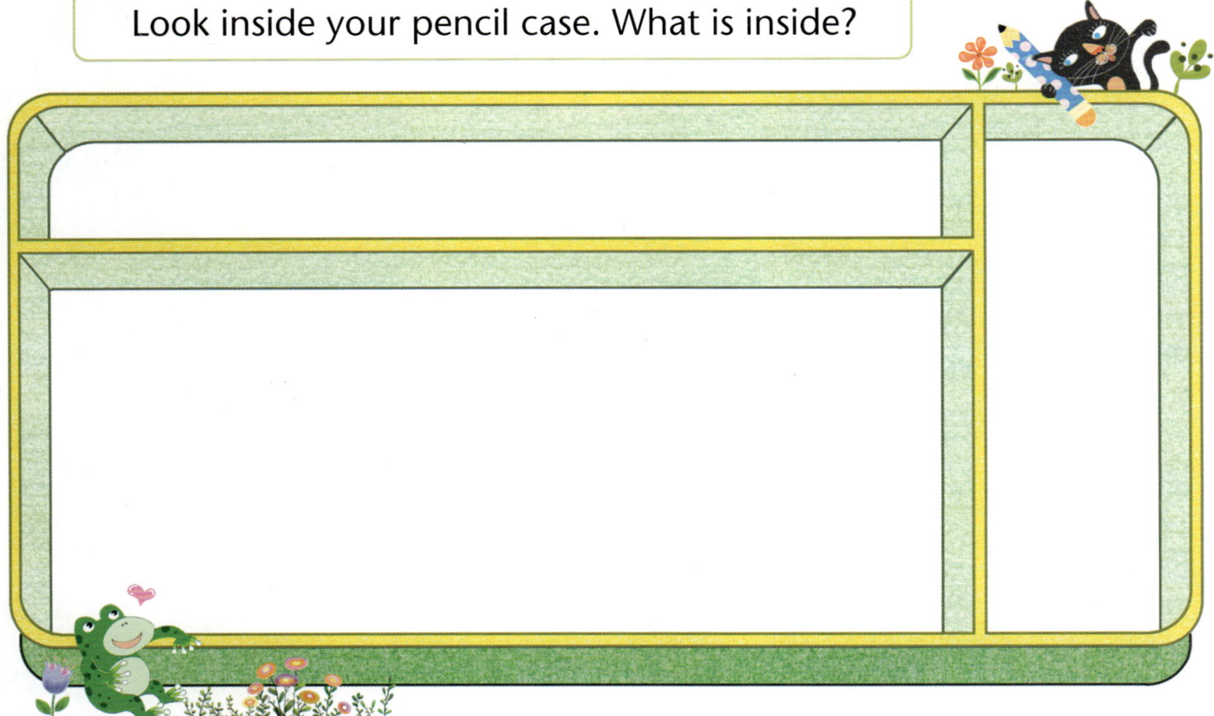

01 The New Baby's Room

T17/20

Mommy, what is that?

It is a **blanket**.

Mommy, what are those?

They are **diapers**.

Mommy, what are these?

They are **bottles**.

Mommy, what is this?

It is a **bed**.

And she is your **new** **baby** sister.

Get Ready

Do you have any brothers or sisters?

Key Words

Listen and point. T18

bed

blanket

new

bottle

diaper

baby

Read and choose.

1. What is the story about?

   a. a baby's blanket   **b.** a baby's bed   **c.** a baby's room

2. Where is the baby?

a.    **b.**    **c.** 

   on the sofa   in the bed   in mom's arms

3. There are ___________ in the baby's room.

   a. balls   **b.** bottles   **c.** teddy bears

Let's Speak

Practice the sentences using the given words.

blanket / diaper / bottle / bed

● **Look, choose and write.**

1. 

2. 

3. 

____

| bed | baby | new | blanket | bottle | diaper |

4. 

5. 

6. 

____

Listening Practice

● **Listen and choose.**  T19

● Look, read and circle.

1.

<u>This</u> / That is a bed.

2.

<u>This</u> / That is a blanket.

3.

<u>These</u> / Those are bottles.

Do It

● Look and choose.

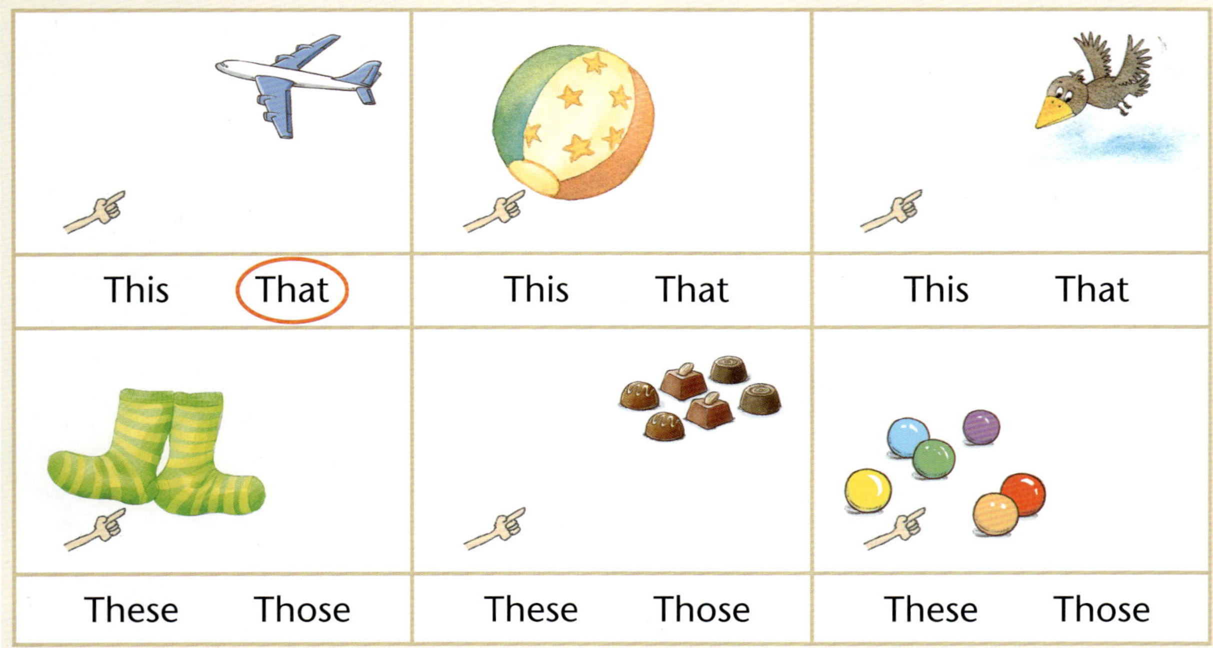

02 My Messy Room

T21/24

The **cookies** are next to the lamp.

The **clock** is in the fishbowl.

The shoes are under the bed.

The **pillows** are on the **floor**.

The **picture** is behind the TV.

The **socks** are ...Uh oh!

Where is my sock?

Key Words

● **Listen and point.** T22

| socks | cookies | picture | clock | pillow | floor |

Read and choose.

1. What is the story about?

    a. a living room   **b.** a kitchen   **c.** a bedroom

2. Where is the clock?

    a.    **b.**    **c.** 

    on the fishbowl   in the fishbowl   next to the fishbowl

3. The boy can't find his ______________ .

    a. cookies   **b.** sock   **c.** TV

Practice the sentences using the given words.

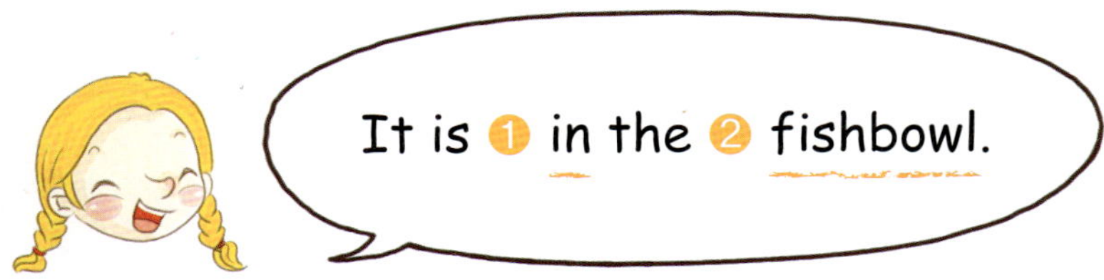

❶ in / on / under / behind / next to

❷ fishbowl / floor / bed / TV / lamp

● **Look and match.**

1. 

2. 

3. 

4. 

5. 

6. 

picture
socks
cookies
floor
clock
pillow

Listening Practice

● **Listen and choose.**  T23

1  O X

2  O X

3  O X

Look, read and circle.

1.    The clock is   **on** / **in**   the fishbowl.

2.    The clock is   **behind** / **next to**   the fishbowl.

3.    The clock is   **in** / **under**   the fishbowl.

Do It

Look, choose and write.

| in | on | under | behind | next to |

The doll is _____________ the table.

The box is _____________ the table.

The balls are _____________ the box.

The mug is _____________ the box.

The spoon is _____________ the box.

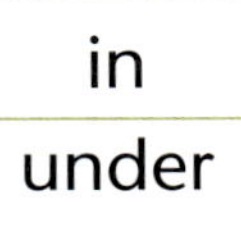

01 School Lockers

T25/28

What's in Mike's locker?

His rollerblades and helmet are in the locker.

What's in Linda's locker?

Her violin is in the locker.

What's in Greg's locker?

His comic books are in the locker.

What's in your locker?

Oh no! My key is in the locker.

Get Ready

What's in your school locker?

Key Words

Listen and point. T26

key

locker

helmet

rollerblade

violin

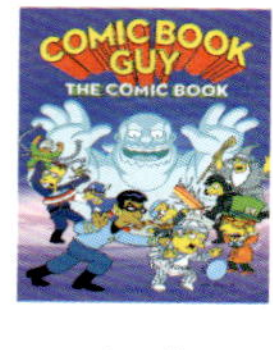

comic book

Read and choose.

1. What is the story about?

    a. a school bus   **b.** a school library   **c.** school lockers

2. What's in Mike's locker?

a.

a helmet

b.

a violin

c.

a key

3. There are _______________ in Greg's locker.

    a. cards   **b.** rollerblades   **c.** comic books

Let's Speak

Practice the sentences using the given words.

❶ His / Her / My
❷ helmet / violin / comic book / key

🟠 **Look and complete.**

1.

k ☐ ☐

2.

h ☐ l ☐ et

3.

☐ oller ☐ lade

4.
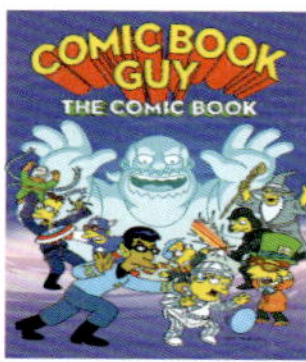
☐ o ☐ ic book

5.

lo ☐ ☐ er

6.

☐ i ☐ lin

Listening Practice

🟠 **Listen and choose.** 

Look, read and circle.

1. 

   Q: What's in Mike's locker?

   A: [He / His]   helmet is in the locker.

2. 

   Q: What's in Linda's locker?

   A: [She / Her]   violin is in the locker.

3. 

   Q: What's in your locker?

   A: [Me / My]   key is in the locker.

Do It

Look, find and tell.

> **EX.**   Ben's bat

The School Fashion Show

T29/32

The fashion show is starting.

Look at Stan!

He is wearing a raincoat and boots.

Look at Sheila!

She is wearing a dress and high heels.

Look at Tom and Amanda!

They are wearing pajamas.

Look at Leo and me!

We are wearing swimsuits and beach hats.

Key Words

● **Listen and point.**  T30

dress

boots

swimsuit

wear

raincoat

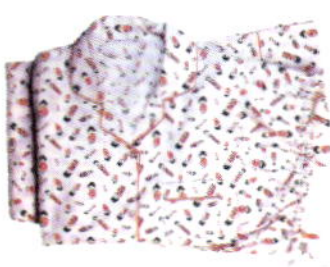
pajamas

Read and choose.

1. What is the story about?

    a. the birthday show   **b.** the fashion show   **c.** the hit show

2. What is Stan wearing?

a. 

raincoat,
boots

b. 

dress,
high heels

c. 

swimsuit,
beach hat

3. _____________ is wearing pajamas.

    a. Sheila   **b.** Amanda   **c.** Leo

Let's Speak

Practice the sentences using the given words.

❶ He / She

❷ a raincoat / boots / a dress / pajamas / a swimsuit / a hat

● **Look and complete.**

1. 
dre☐☐

2. 
swi☐sui☐

3. 
b☐☐ts

4. 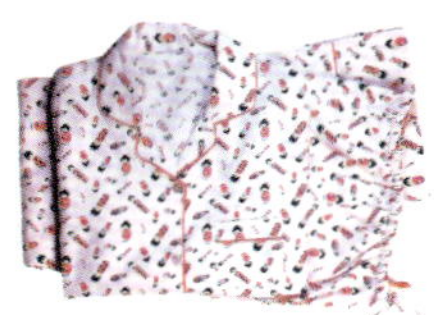
p☐☐amas

5. 
w☐☐r

6. 
r☐in☐oat

● **Listen and choose.**  T31

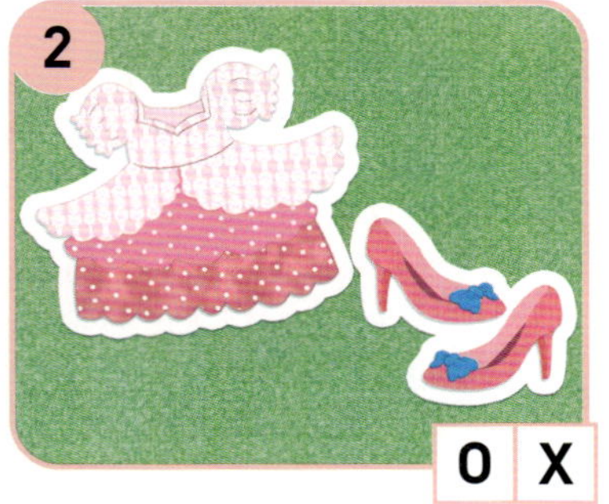

🟠 **Look, read and circle.**

1. 
He is wear / **is wearing** a raincoat.

2. 
She wearing / **is wearing** a dress.

3. 
We wears / **are wearing** pajamas.

Do It

🟠 **Draw, color and write.**

01 Let's Play Together

T33/36

I have some dolls.

Rebecca doesn't have any.

I have some blocks and puzzles.

Rebecca doesn't have any.

I have some cards.

Rebecca doesn't have any.

I have some friends.

Rebecca doesn't have any.

Let's play together, Rebecca!

Get Ready

What do you do for fun with your friends?

Key Words

Listen and point. T34

puzzle

doll

play

friend

card

block

● **Read and choose.**

1. What is the story about?

   a. studying together   **b.** playing together   **c.** living together

2. What do 'I' have?

   a. 

   some dolls

   b. 

   some toy cars

   c. 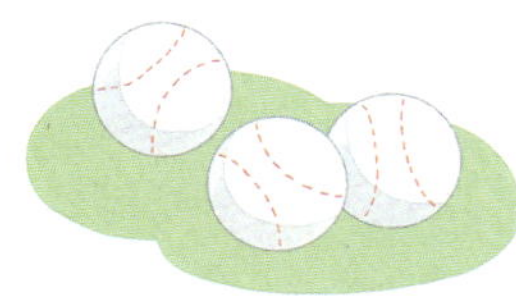

   some balls

3. What does Rebecca have now?

   a. some dolls   **b.** some yo-yos   **c.** some friends

● **Practice the sentences using the given words.**

dolls / blocks / puzzles / cards / friends

● **Look, choose and write.**

1.

2.

3.

card   puzzle   doll   play   block   friend

4.

5.

6.

Listening Practice

● **Listen and choose.** 

Look, read and circle.

1.  I | have some / don't have any | cards.

2.  I | have some / don't have any | friends.

3.  She | has some / doesn't have any | dolls.

Do you have any of these in your backpack? Write and tell.

I have some ______________.

I don't have any ______________.

02 Jacob and I

Jacob and I are best friends.

We never stay home.

We always ride bikes.

We usually go to the park.

We sometimes play tag.

We sometimes jump rope.

We sometimes play soccer.

We sometimes fight, too.

But we always say, "I'm sorry."

Who is your best friend?

Key Words

Listen and point. 

fight

ride

home

bike

soccer

park

Read and choose.

1. What is the story about?

    a. my best friend   **b.** my lovely family   **c.** my funny teacher

2. What do Jacob and I always do?

    a.   **b.**   **c.**

    ride bikes   play soccer   fight

3. What do Jacob and I always say after fighting?

    a. "Let's stay home."   **b.** "I don't like you."   **c.** "I'm sorry."

Practice the sentences using the given words.

    ① never / always / usually / sometimes

    ② stay home / ride bikes / go to the park / play tag / jump rope / play soccer / fight

● **Look and match.**

1. 

2. 

bike

fight

home

park

ride

soccer

3. 

4. 

5. 

6.

● **Listen and number the pictures.**  T39

● **Look, read and circle.**

1.

We $\dfrac{\text{always}}{\text{sometimes}}$ ride bikes.

2.
We $\dfrac{\text{sometimes}}{\text{never}}$ stay home.

3.
We $\dfrac{\text{sometimes}}{\text{never}}$ fight.

● **Look, choose and write. How often do you do these things?**

UNIT 6 01

At a Flower Garden

T41/44

What do you see?

I see one yellow flower.

It is a sunflower.

What do you see?

I see three white flowers.

They are lilies.

What do you see?

Oh! I see one insect.

It is a honeybee. Bzzz.

Get Ready

What kind of things do you see in the garden?

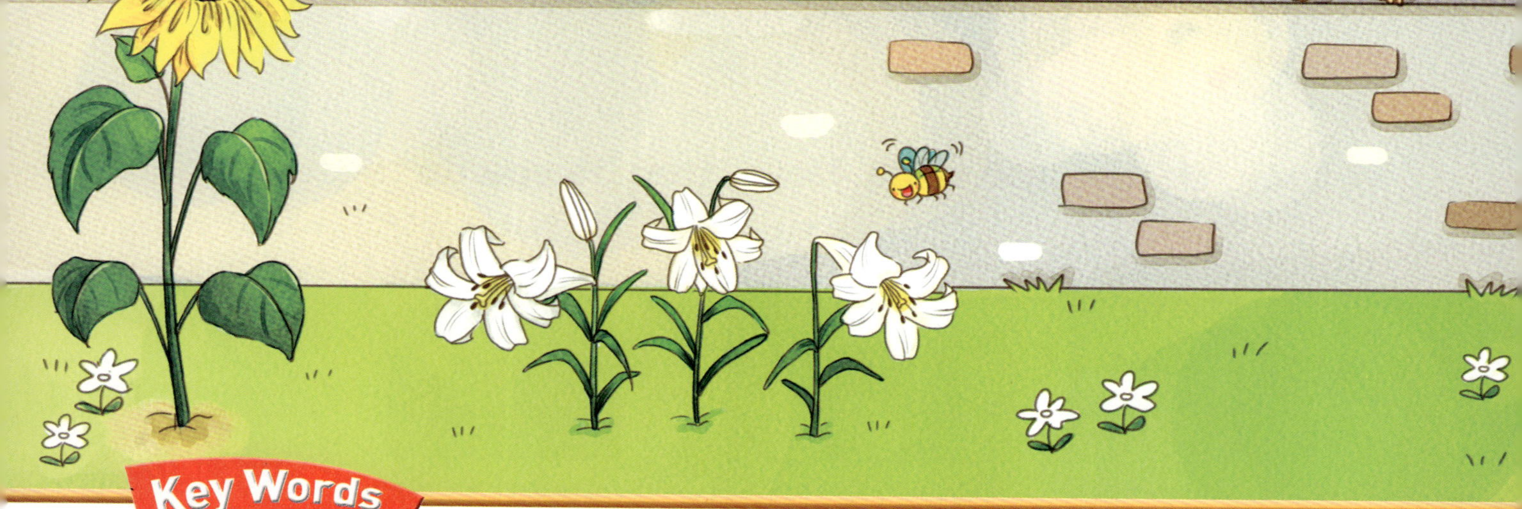

Key Words

Listen and point. T42

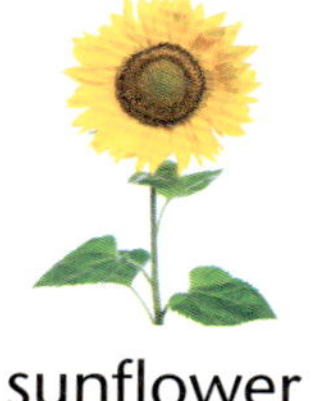

sunflower

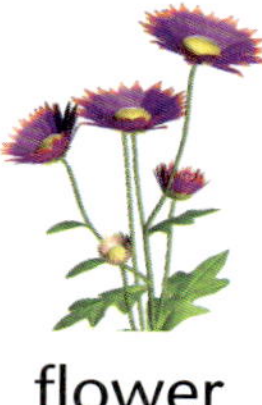

flower

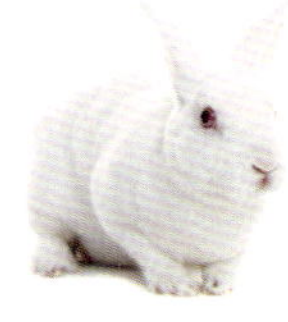

white

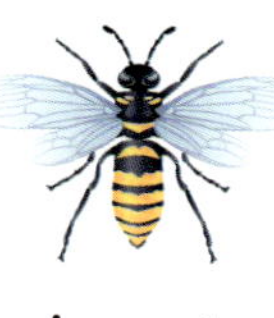

insect

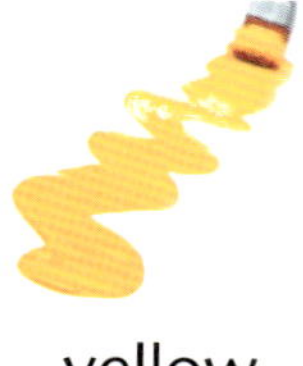

yellow

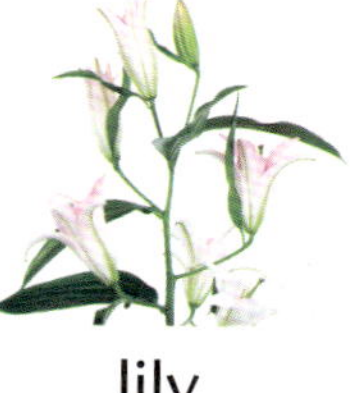

lily

Read and choose.

1. What is the story about?

    a. a honeybee   **b.** many flowers   **c.** a flower garden

2. What flowers does the boy not see?

    a. 

a sunflower

    b. 

lilies

    c. 

tulips

3. The insect is a _______________ .

    a. honeybee   **b.** ladybug   **c.** spider

Let's Speak

Practice the sentences using the given words.

❶ a sunflower / a lily / an insect

❷ sunflowers / lilies / insects

🟠 **Look, choose and write.**

1. 

2. 

3. 

| lily | insect | flower | white | yellow | sunflower |

4. 

5. 

6. 

Listening Practice

🟠 **Listen and choose.** 

1   O   X

2   O   X

3   O   X

Look, read and circle.

1. 

   I see a yellow flower. **It is / They are** a sunflower.

2. 

   I see white flowers. **It is / They are** lilies.

3.

   I see an insect. **It is / They are** a honeybee.

Do It

What do you see in the box? Talk about them.

| toy car | robot | yo-yo | kite | stuffed animal |

What Plants Need

T45/48

Jane needs water.

Plants need water, too.

Jane needs air.

Plants need air, too.

Jane needs food.

Plants need food, too.

But plants don't need meat and vegetables.

Plants need sunlight.

With water, air, and sunlight, plants grow.

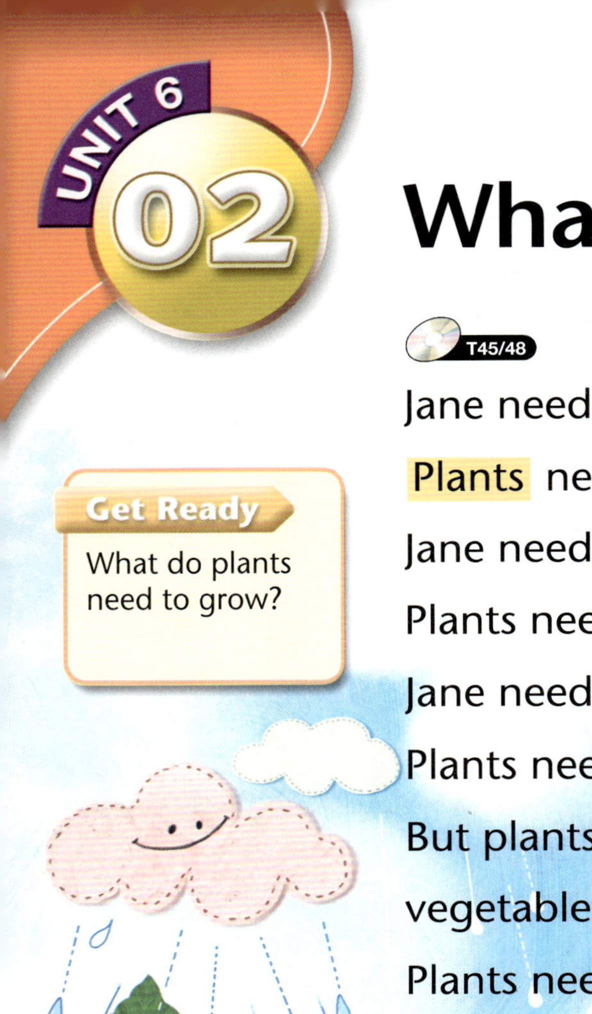

Key Words

● **Listen and point.** T46

sunlight

water

food

plant

air

grow

Read and choose.

1. What is the story about?

    a. food   **b.** sunlight   **c.** plants

2. What do plants not need?

    a. 
    b. 
    c. 

    meat   sunlight   water

3. Without water, air, and sunlight, plants won't ____________.

    a. eat   **b.** grow   **c.** die

Let's Speak

Practice the sentences using the given words.

❶ water / air / food

● **Look and complete.**

1. 

wa ☐☐ r

2. 

☐☐ r

3. 

pl ☐☐ t

4. 

sunli ☐☐ t

5. 

gr ☐☐

6. 

f ☐☐ d

● **Listen and number the pictures.**  T47

Look, read and circle.

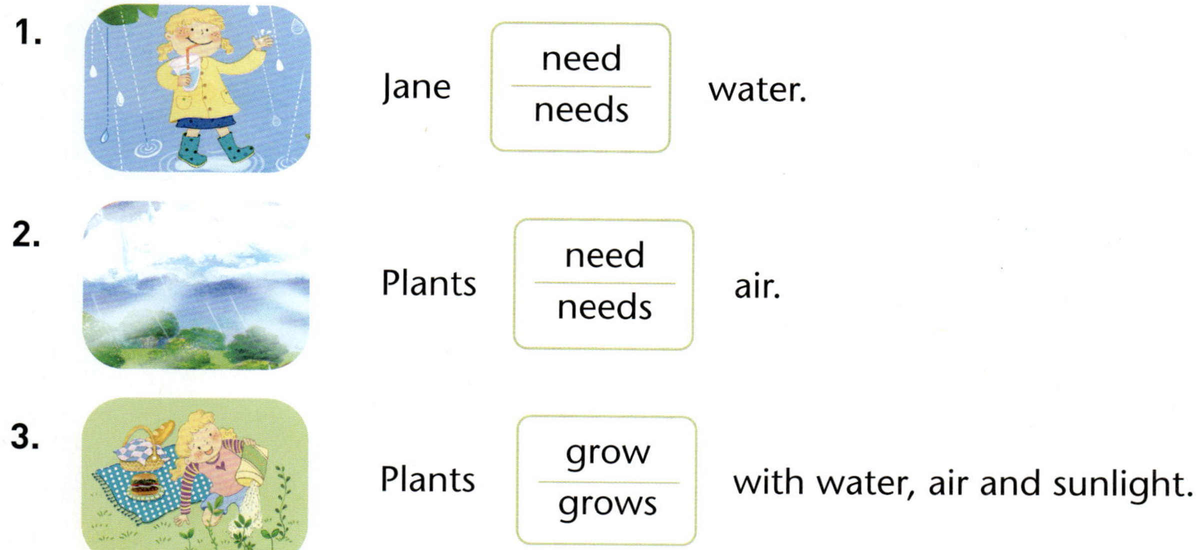

1. Jane
   need / needs
   water.

2. Plants
   need / needs
   air.

3. Plants
   grow / grows
   with water, air and sunlight.

Draw your favorite flower and what it needs. Then complete the crossword.

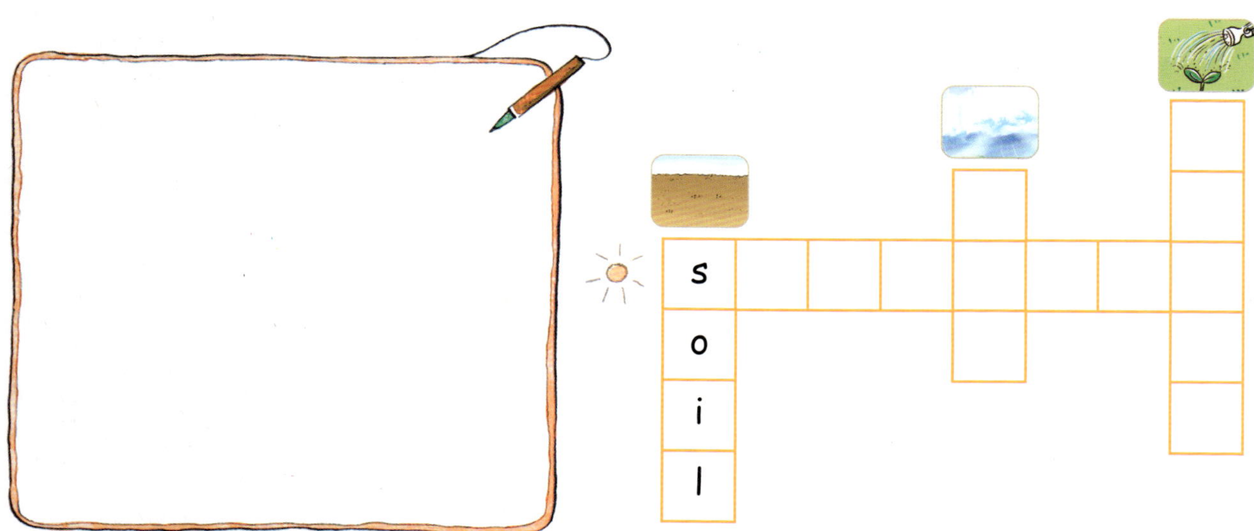

Goldfish Facts

T49/52

Do you know about goldfish?

Goldfish eat fish and vegetables.

But they don't eat spaghetti.

Goldfish sleep.

But they don't sleep in beds.

Goldfish live in water.

But they don't live in pools.

Goldfish play together.

But they don't play with sharks.

What do you know about goldfish?

Key Words

● **Listen and point.**  T50

vegetable

fish

shark

sleep

eat

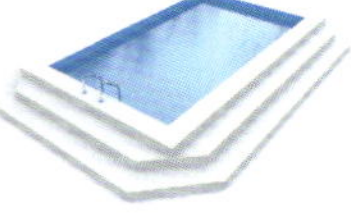

pool

● **Read and choose.**

1. **What is the story about?**

   a. goldfish

   b. goldfish in pools

   c. goldfish and sharks

2. **What do goldfish not eat?**

   a. 
   fish

   b. 
   vegetable

   c. 
   spaghetti

3. **Goldfish play with ____________ .**

   a. toys   **b.** goldfish   **c.** sharks

Let's Speak

● **Practice the sentences using the given words.**

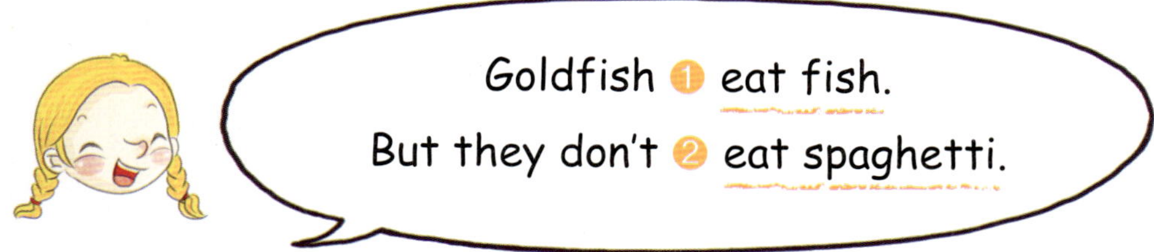

❶ **eat fish** / sleep / live in water / play together

❷ **eat spaghetti** / sleep in beds / live in pools / play with sharks

🟠 **Look, choose and write.**

1. 

2. 

3. 

____

eat   pool   fish   sleep   vegetable   shark

4. 

5. 

6. 

Listening Practice

🟠 **Listen and choose.** T51

1

O | X

2

O | X

3

O | X

Look, read and circle.

1.  Goldfish [eat / don't eat] vegetables.

2. Goldfish [live / don't live] in pools.

3. Goldfish [play / don't play] with sharks.

Look and match. Where do they live?

02

What a Funny Bird!

T53/56

My **bird**, Coco, is **funny**.

She doesn't live in a **cage**.

She lives in a dog house.

She doesn't **sing** songs.

She **listens** to jazz.

She doesn't eat **worms**.

She eats garlic bread.

Coco doesn't do bird things.

But I love my funny bird!

Key Words

● **Listen and point.** **T54**

worm

listen

bird

sing

funny

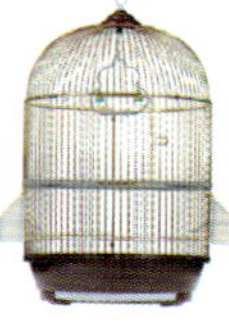

cage

● **Read and choose.**

1. What is the story about?

   a. a pet bird   **b.** a funny song   **c.** strange worms

2. What does Coco eat?

   a.

worms

   b.

garlic bread

   c.

seeds

3. Coco is a ______________ bird.

   a. cute   **b.** busy   **c.** funny

Let's Speak

● **Practice the sentences using the given words.**

❶ live in a cage / sing songs / eat worms
❷ lives in a dog house / listens to jazz / eats garlic bread

● **Look and match.**

1. 

2. 

3. 

4. 

5. 

6. 

- listen
- worm
- bird
- funny
- sing
- cage

Listening Practice

● **Listen and choose.** T55

1 　O　X

2 　O　X

3 　O　X

- **Look, read and circle.**

1.  She | lives / doesn't live | in a dog house.

2. She | sings / doesn't sing | songs.

3.  She | eats / doesn't eat | garlic bread.

- **Look. Fill in the missing letters in pet words.**

01 What a Bad Day!

It is windy today.

The **wind** is blowing my **hair**.

It is cloudy today.

The **clouds** are **hiding** the sun.

It is rainy today.

The **rain** is falling on my **face**.

It is a bad day today.

How's the weather tomorrow?

Get Ready

How is the weather today?

Key Words

● **Listen and point.** T58

rain

face

cloud

hide

wind

hair

- **Read and choose.**

1. **What is the story about?**

   a. a bad day　　　　**b.** a lucky day　　　　**c.** a sunny day

2. **What are the clouds hiding?**

   a. 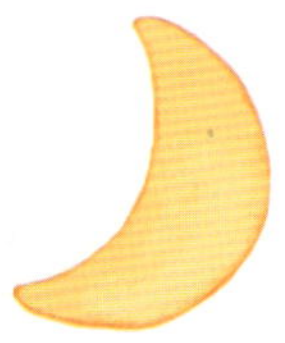　　　**b.** 　　　**c.** 

   the moon　　　　　　the star　　　　　　the sun

3. **The** ______________ **is falling on the boy's face.**

   a. rain　　　　　　**b.** snow　　　　　　**c.** wind

Let's Speak

- **Practice the sentences using the given words.**

windy / cloudy / rainy

- **Look, unscramble and write.**

1. 

____

ndiw

2. 

____

eihd

3. 

____

nair

4. 

____

arhi

5. 

____

lcdou

6. 

____

acef

- **Listen and choose.**  T59

1. 

2. 

3. 

Look, read and circle.

1. It is ~~wind~~ / **windy** today.

2. It is ~~cloud~~ / **cloudy** today.

3. It is ~~rain~~ / **rainy** today.

Look and tell.

02 Safe in the Sun

T61/64

Do you wear sunscreen?

Do you wear a hat?

Do you wear sunglasses?

Do you drink water?

Do you sit and rest?

Let's answer, "Yes, I do!"

And stay safe in the sun.

Key Words

● **Listen and point.** T62

sunglasses   hat   drink   safe   rest   sunscreen

Read and choose.

1. What is the story about?

   a. food safety   **b.** sun safety   **c.** street safety

2. What do you need to wear in the sun?

  a.    **b.**    **c.** 

   sunscreen, hat, sunglasses   sunscreen, glasses, scarf   sunglasses, swimsuit, hat

3. We have to stay safe in the _____________ .

  a. sun   **b.** night   **c.** water

Practice the sentences using the given words.

sunscreen / a hat / sunglasses

● **Look and complete.**

1. 

h□□

2. 

d□i□k

3. 

sunscr□□n

4. 

sungla□□es

5. 

□es□

6. 

s□f□

Listening Practice

● **Listen and choose.** T63

1

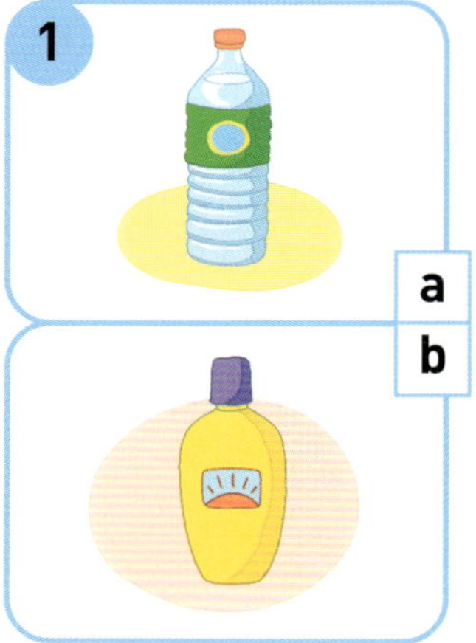

2

3

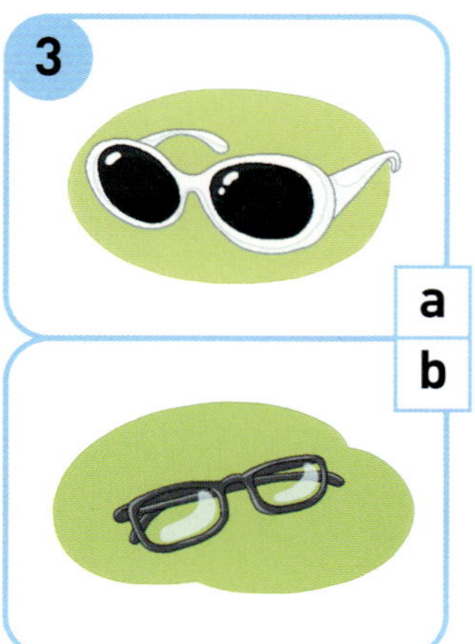

Look, read and circle.

1.

Q: Do you wear sunscreen?

A: Yes, I do. / No, I don't.

2.

Q: Do you wear sunglasses?

A: Yes, I do. / No, I don't.

3.

Q: Do you wear a hat?

A: Yes, I do. / No, I don't.

Answer the questions.

At the Beach

	Yes, I do.	No, I don't.
1. Do you wear sunscreen?	☐	☐
2. Do you wear a hat?	☐	☐
3. Do you wear sunglasses?	☐	☐
4. Do you drink water?	☐	☐
5. Do you wear glasses?	☐	☐

01

My Senses

T65/68

My ears can hear.

But they can't smell.

My nose can smell.

But it can't see.

My eyes can see.

But they can't taste.

My mouth can taste.

But it can't hear!

Key Words

● **Listen and point.** T66

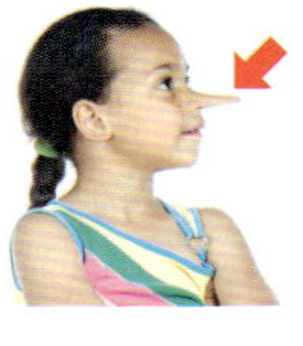

nose

hear

ear

taste

smell

mouth

● **Read and choose.**

1. What is the story about?

   a. ears
   b. eyes
   c. face

2. What can he hear with?

   a. 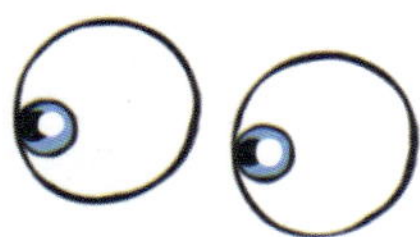
   b. 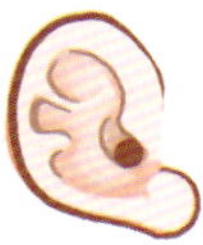
   c. 

   his eyes
   his ears
   his mouth

3. He can ______________ with his eyes.

   a. smell
   b. see
   c. taste

● **Practice the sentences using the given words.**

❶ ears / nose / eyes / mouth
❷ hear / smell / see / taste

Look, choose and write.

1. 

2. 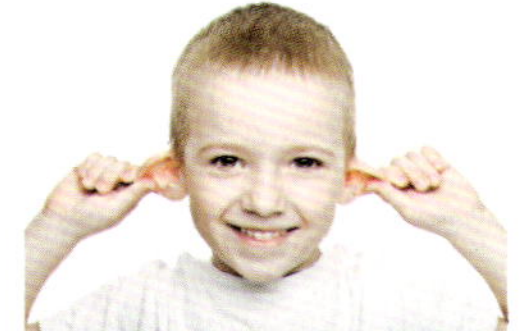

3. 

| mouth | hear | nose | smell | ear | taste |

4. 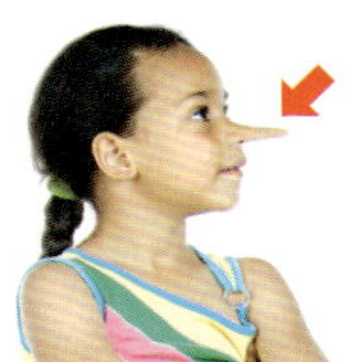

5. 

6. 

Listening Practice

Listen and choose. 

1 

a b

2 

a b

3 

a b

● Look, read and circle.

1. My mouth can / can't hear.

2. My nose can / can't smell.

3. My eyes can / can't see.

Do It

● Look and complete.

02

Clean Hands, Healthy Hands

T69/72

It's time for dinner.

You need to wash your hands.

First, wet your hands with water.

Next, put some soap on your hands.

Then, rub your hands together.

Wash between your fingers, too!

Finally, rinse and dry your hands.

Now, they are clean.

Let's eat!

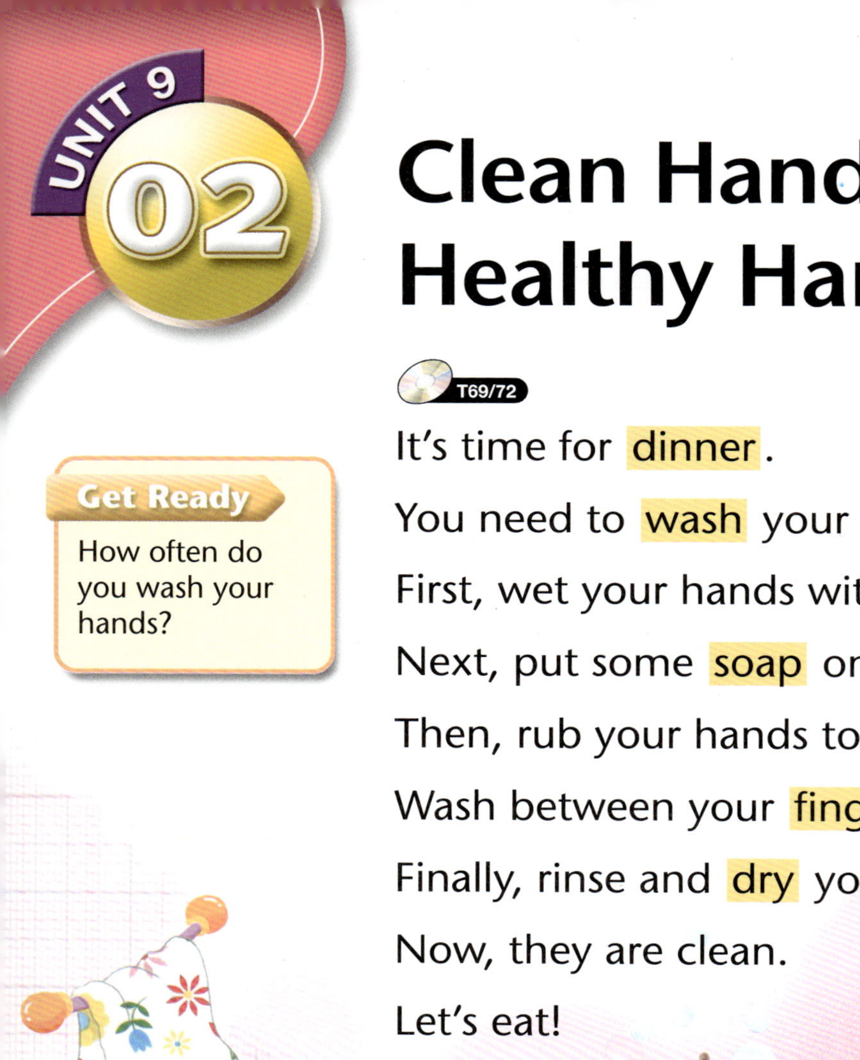

Key Words

● **Listen and point.** T70

wash

hand

dinner

finger

soap

dry

Read and choose.

1. What is the story about?

   a. hair washing   **b.** hand washing   **c.** foot washing

2. What do we wash our hands with?

   a.

   b.

   c.

towel and water   soap and water   hand dryer and water

3. We wash our hands before we ______________ .

   a. eat   **b.** sleep   **c.** talk

Let's Speak

Practice the sentences using the given words.

> wet your hands with water / rub your hands together
> wash between your fingers / rinse and dry your hands

🟠 **Look and match.**

1.

2.

| hand |
| dinner |
| wash |
| soap |
| finger |
| dry |

3.

4.

5.

6.

🟠 **Listen and number the pictures.** 

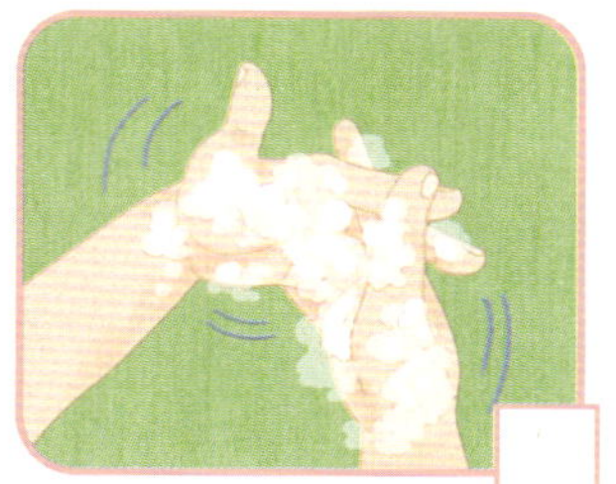

Look, read and circle.

1.

Wet
Dry

your hands with water.

2.

Rub
Put

your hands together.

3.

Dry
Rinse

your hands.

Number the pictures in the order you wash your hands.

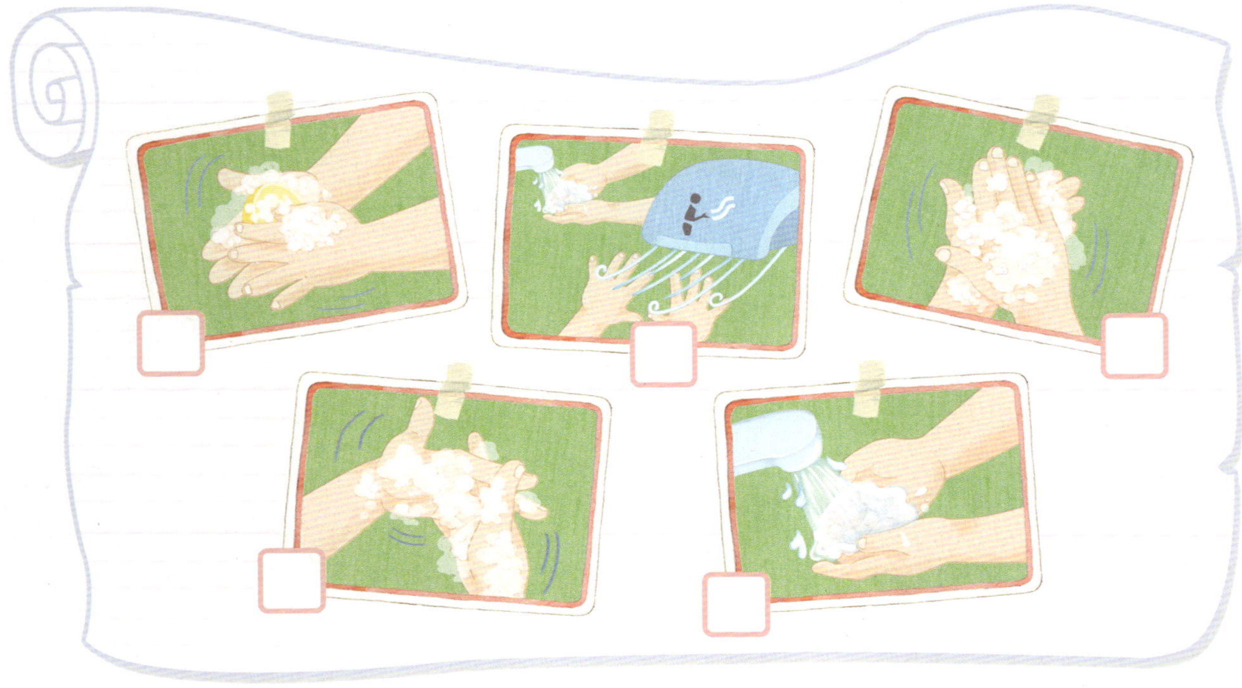

01 At the Zoo

T73/76

The penguins don't have coats.

Are they cold?

No, they aren't.

The lion doesn't have a flashlight.

Is it scared?

No, it isn't.

The dolphins don't have boats.

Are they tired?

No, they aren't.

But I am!

Key Words

● **Listen and point.**  T74

cold

dolphin

tired

boat

lion

scared

Read and choose.

1. What is the story about?
   - **a.** penguins at the zoo
   - **b.** lions at the zoo
   - **c.** animals at the zoo

2. What is not scared?

   a. 

   the penguins

   b. 

   the lion

   c. 

   the dolphins

3. The boy feels ______________ .
   - **a.** sad
   - **b.** tired
   - **c.** excited

Practice the sentences using the given words.

cold / scared / tired

⦿ **Look, unscramble and write.**

1. 

odcl

2. 

niol

3. 

edrsca

4. 

phdolin

5. 

idetr

6. 

btao

Listening Practice

⦿ **Listen and choose.**  T75

1. 
O | X

2. 
O | X

3. 
O | X

Look, read and circle.

1. 

   Q: Is / Are they cold?

   A: No, they aren't.

2. 

   Q: Is it scared?

   A: No, it is / isn't .

3. 

   Q: Are they tired?

   A: No, they are / aren't .

Help Pooh find its home.

UNIT 10
02 Sick Day

T77/80

I am feeling sick today.

I am staying in bed.

My mom is bringing soup.

But I'm not eating.

My mom is bringing milk.

But I'm not drinking.

My mom is bringing books.

But I'm not reading.

I am just sleeping and sleeping.

Get Ready

What do you do when you feel sick?

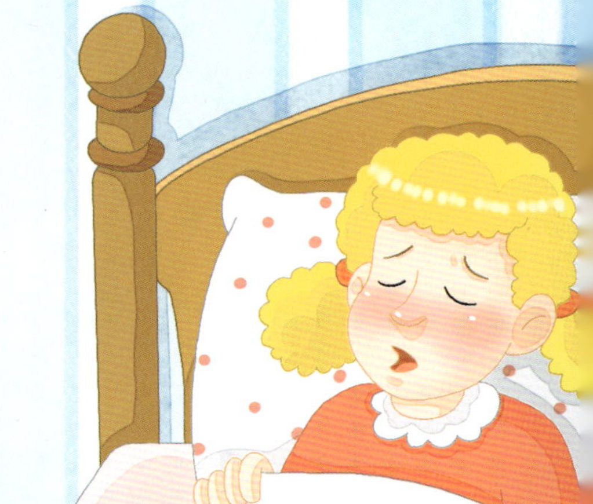

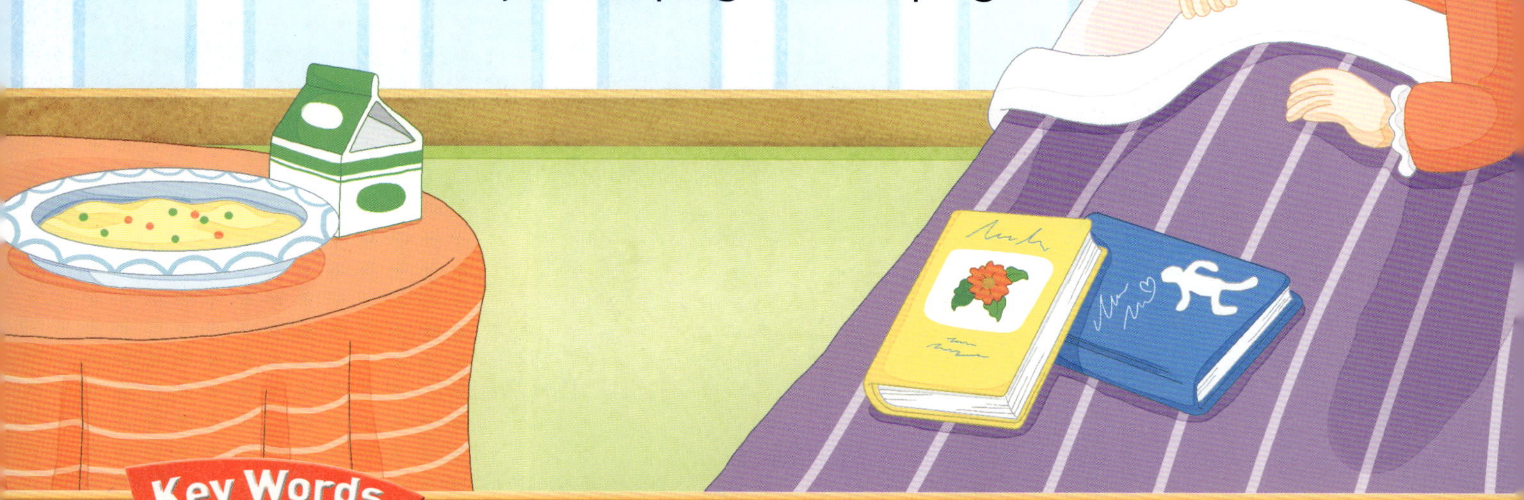

Key Words

Listen and point. T78

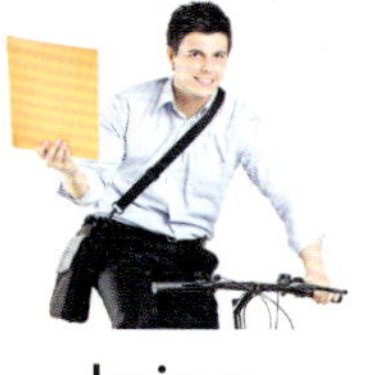

bring

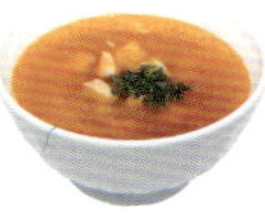

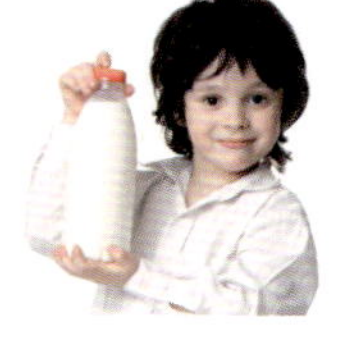

soup

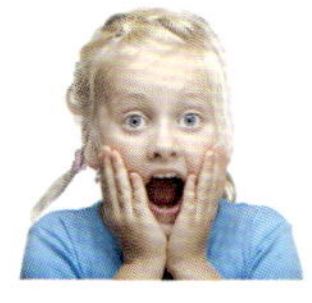

milk

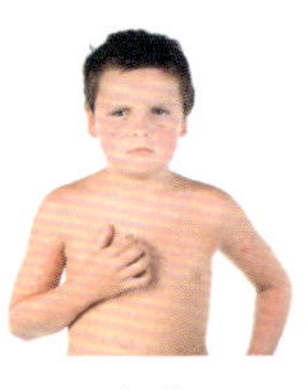

feel

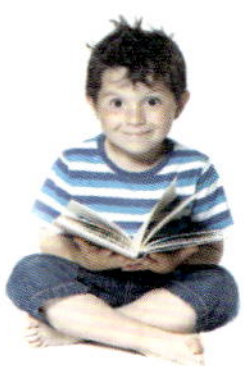

sick

read

Read and choose.

1. What is the story about?

    a. feeling happy   **b.** feeling sick   **c.** feeling tired

2. What is the girl's mom bringing?

a.

soup, milk and books

b.

pancakes, syrup and water

c.

cookies, milk and soup

3. The girl is just ______________ .

    a. eating   **b.** drinking   **c.** sleeping

Let's Speak

Practice the sentences using the given words.

❶ soup / milk / books

❷ eating / drinking / reading

- **Look and complete.**

1. 

s⬜⬜p

2. 

r⬜⬜d

3. 

bri⬜⬜

4. 

f⬜⬜l

5. 

mi⬜⬜

6. 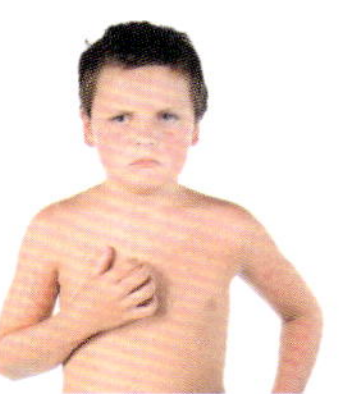

si⬜⬜

- **Listen and choose.**  T79

Look, read and circle.

1. 

I am feeling sick today. I am [stay / staying] in bed.

2. 

My mom is bringing soup. I [don't / am not] eating.

3.

My mom is bringing books. I am [reading not / not reading] .

What is he or she doing? Number and tell.

① drawing ② running ③ singing ④ drinking ⑤ riding
⑥ sleeping ⑦ eating ⑧ studying ⑨ reading ⑩ cleaning

MEMO

Reading
Start
1
Workbook
WorldCom ELT

Reading Start

1

Workbook

WorldCom ELT

My Monster Family

Word Review Find and circle.

1 mom

2 brother

3 family

4 name

5 dad

6 sister

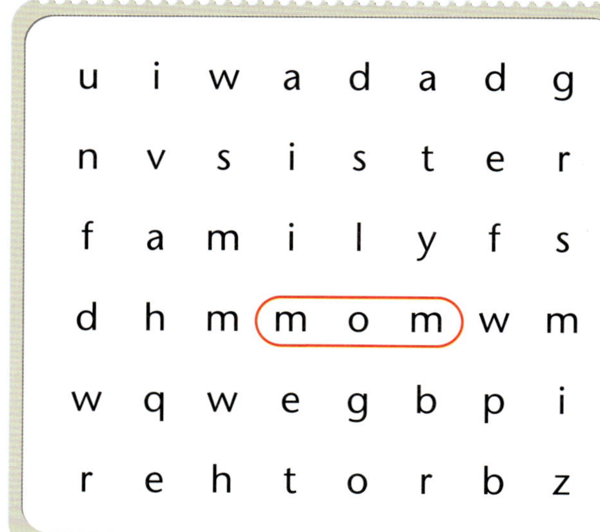

u	i	w	a	d	a	d	g
n	v	s	i	s	t	e	r
f	a	m	i	l	y	f	s
d	h	m	m	o	m	w	m
w	q	w	e	g	b	p	i
r	e	h	t	o	r	b	z

Grammar Practice Choose and write.

1.  ______________ ______________ my dad.

2.  ______________ ______________ my mom.

3.  ______________ ______________ my brother and sister.

I am
He is
She is
They are

2

1. Spook / name / My / is / .

2. a monster family / are / We / .

3. hello / to my dad / Say / .

Dictation Listen and fill in the blanks. 

Boo! My _______________ is Spook.

I am a ghost.

Say hello to my dad.

He is a zombie.

Say hello to my _______________ .

She is a witch.

Say hello to my _______________ and sister.

They are vampires.

We are a _______________ family.

A Royal Family

Word Review Do the crossword.

Grammar Practice Choose and write.

1.

Q: _____________ is he?

A: He is my father.

2.

Q: Who is _____________?

A: She is my mother.

3.

Q: Who are they?

A: _____________ _____________ my brothers.

Who
she
I am
They are

Writing Practice Unscramble and write.

1. is / he / Who / ?

2. Princess Jam / am / I / .

3. in / live / We / Sandwich Land / .

Dictation Listen and fill in the blanks. 

Who is he?

He is my father, King Butter.

_______________ is she?

She is my mother, Queen _______________ .

Who are they?

They are my brothers, Prince Knife and Prince _______________ .

Who are you?

I am Princess _______________ .

Together, we live in Sandwich Land.

01 My Robot, Turbo!

Word Review Choose and complete.

1. 

st⬜ong

2. 

ro⬜ot

3. 

smar⬜

e   r   a   t   b   l

4. 

f⬜st

5. 

a⬜ien

6. 

h⬜ro

Grammar Practice Read and write.

1. 

Turbo is ____________.
He flies to the moon.

2. 

Turbo is ____________.
He reads big books.

3. 

Turbo is ____________.
He fights scary aliens.

smart
fast
strong
great

1. is / my / Turbo / robot / .

2. books / He / big / reads / .

3. hero / Turbo / my / is / .

Dictation Listen and fill in the blanks. T12

Turbo is my _________________.

Turbo is fast.

He flies to the _______________.

Turbo is smart.

He reads big books.

Turbo is strong.

He fights scary aliens.

Turbo is _______________!

Turbo is my _______________.

02 My Fun Stickers

Word Review Circle and match.

1. 

2. 

3. 

s t a r c o l o r f u l s t i c k e r s h a r p r a b b i t p e n c i l

4. 

5. 

6. 

Grammar Practice Read and choose.

1. 

_______________ a vanilla cupcake.

a. There is 　　　　　　　**b.** There are

2. 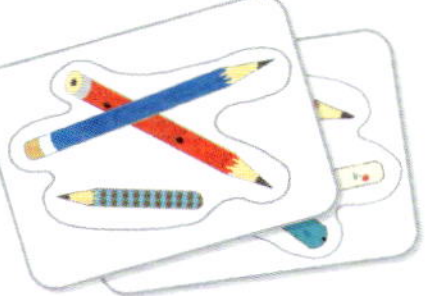

_______________ sharp pencils.

a. There is 　　　　　　　**b.** There are

3. 

_______________ a pretty mermaid.

a. There is 　　　　　　　**b.** There are

Writing Practice **Unscramble and write.**

1. are / sparkly stars / There / .

2. is / a fuzzy rabbit / There / .

3. ten / I / more / want / .

Dictation **Listen and fill in the blanks.** 

There are ________________ stickers in my sticker book.

There are sparkly ________________.

There is a vanilla cupcake.

There are colorful racecars.

There is a fuzzy ________________.

There are sharp pencils.

There is a ________________ mermaid.

And I ________________ ten more!

01 The New Baby's Room

Word Review Find and circle.

1 
bed

2 
blanket

3 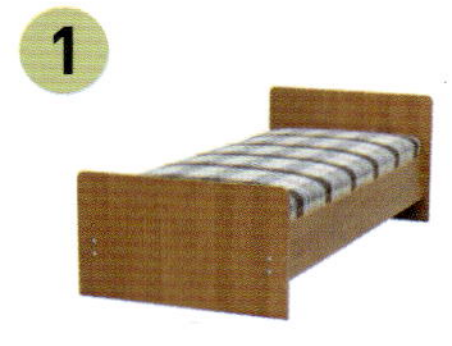
new

4 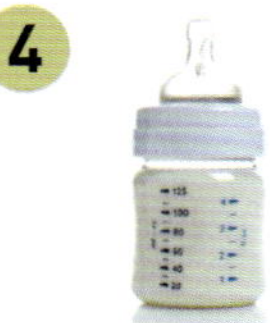
bottle

5 
baby

6 
diaper

p	g	i	l	f	e	e	a
u	h	e	b	e	d	l	r
d	i	a	p	e	r	t	s
b	l	a	n	k	e	t	t
h	d	y	b	a	b	o	f
h	k	c	n	e	w	b	n

Grammar Practice Look, choose and write.

1. 
Q: What _____________ _____________ ?
A: It is a blanket.

2. 
Q: What _____________ _____________ ?
A: They are diapers.

3. 
Q: What _____________ _____________ ?
A: They are bottles.

is this
is that
are these
are those

Writing Practice Unscramble and write.

1. that / What / is / ?

2. a blanket / is / It / .

3. is / your / new baby sister / She / .

Dictation Listen and fill in the blanks. 

Mommy, what is ________________?

It is a blanket.

Mommy, what are those?

They are diapers.

Mommy, what are ________________?

They are bottles.

Mommy, what is ________________?

It is a bed.

And she is your new ________________ sister.

02 My Messy Room

Word Review Do the crossword.

Grammar Practice Choose and write.

1.  The clock is ______________ the fishbowl.

2. The shoes are ______________ the bed.

3.  The picture is ______________ the TV.

on
in
under
behind

Writing Practice Unscramble and write.

1. are / the lamp / The cookies / next to / .

2. on / the floor / The pillows / are / .

3. is / Where / my sock / ?

Dictation Listen and fill in the blanks. 

The cookies are next to the ________________ .

The clock is in the fishbowl.

The ________________ are under the bed.

The pillows are on the floor.

The ________________ is behind the TV.

The socks are ··· Uh oh!

Where is my ________________ ?

01 School Lockers

Word Review Choose and complete.

1. ☐elmet

2. roller☐lade

3. ☐iolin

| b | e | h | v | c | m |

4. k☐y

5. lo☐ker

6. co☐ic book

Grammar Practice Look, choose and write.

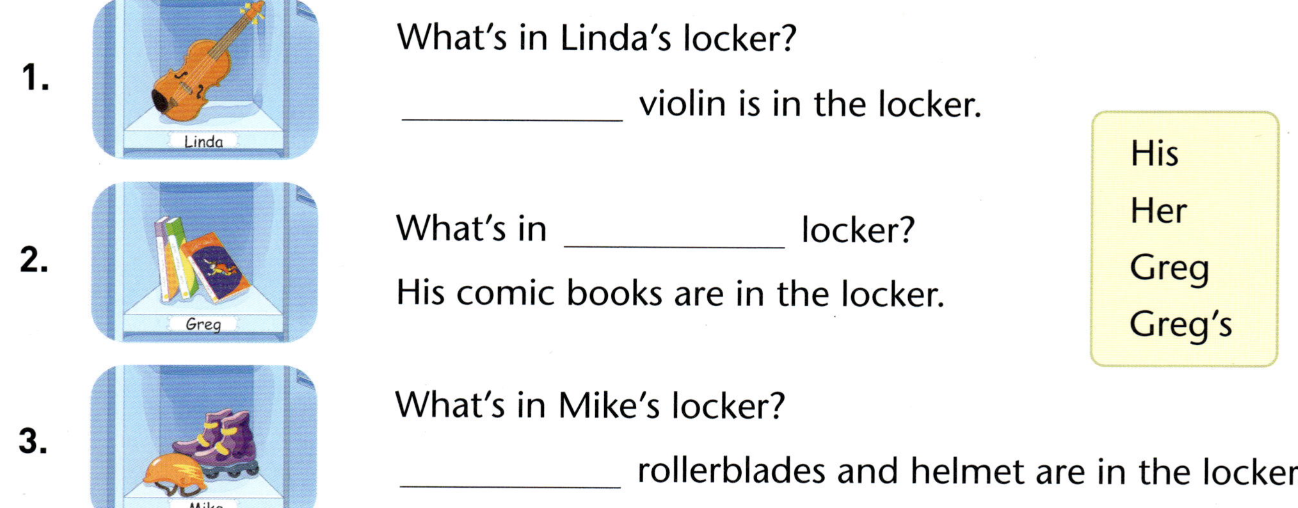

1. What's in Linda's locker?

_____________ violin is in the locker.

2. What's in _____________ locker?
His comic books are in the locker.

3. What's in Mike's locker?

_____________ rollerblades and helmet are in the locker.

His
Her
Greg
Greg's

Writing Practice Unscramble and write.

1. in / Her violin / the locker / is / .

2. in / locker / What's / your / ?

3. the locker / My key / in / is / .

Dictation Listen and fill in the blanks. 

What's in Mike's locker?

His rollerblades and _______________ are in the locker.

What's in Linda's locker?

Her _______________ is in the locker.

What's in Greg's locker?

His _______________ _______________ are in the locker.

What's in your locker?

Oh no! My _______________ is in the locker.

02 The School Fashion Show

Word Review Circle and match.

1. 

2. 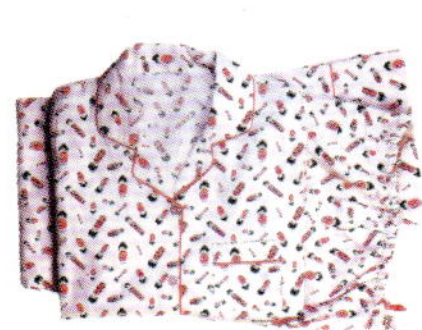

3. 

p a j a m a s w e a r d r e s s r a i n c o a t b o o t s s w i m s u i t

4. 

5. 

6. 

Grammar Practice Read and match.

1.    They are wearing pajamas.

2.    He is wearing a raincoat.

3.    She is wearing a dress.

Writing Practice Unscramble and write.

1. is / starting / The fashion show / .

2. are / pajamas / They / wearing / .

3. at / Leo and me / Look / !

Dictation Listen and fill in the blanks. 

The ________________ show is starting.

Look at Stan!

He is ________________ a raincoat and boots.

Look at Sheila!

She is wearing a dress and high heels.

Look at Tom and Amanda!

They are wearing ________________.

Look at Leo and me!

We are wearing ________________ and beach hats.

01 Let's Play Together

Word Review Find and circle.

1 
card

3 
doll

5 
friend

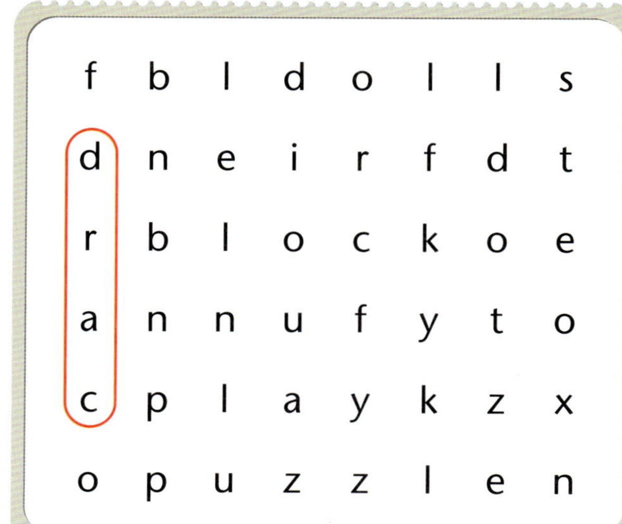

2 
puzzle

4 
play

6
block

Grammar Practice Read and circle.

1.  I have (some / any) dolls.

2.  I have (some / any) blocks and puzzles.

3. Rebecca doesn't have (some / any) cards.

1. some / I / friends / have / .

2. doesn't / any / Rebecca / have / .

3. together / Let's / play / !

Dictation Listen and fill in the blanks. 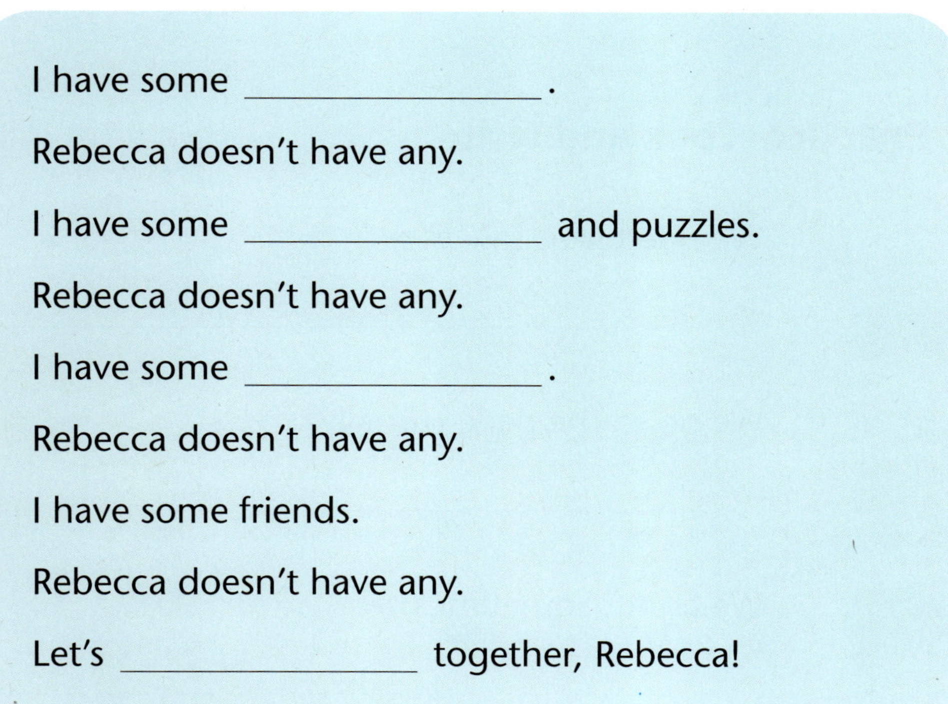

I have some _______________ .

Rebecca doesn't have any.

I have some _______________ and puzzles.

Rebecca doesn't have any.

I have some _______________ .

Rebecca doesn't have any.

I have some friends.

Rebecca doesn't have any.

Let's _______________ together, Rebecca!

Jacob and I

Word Review Do the crossword.

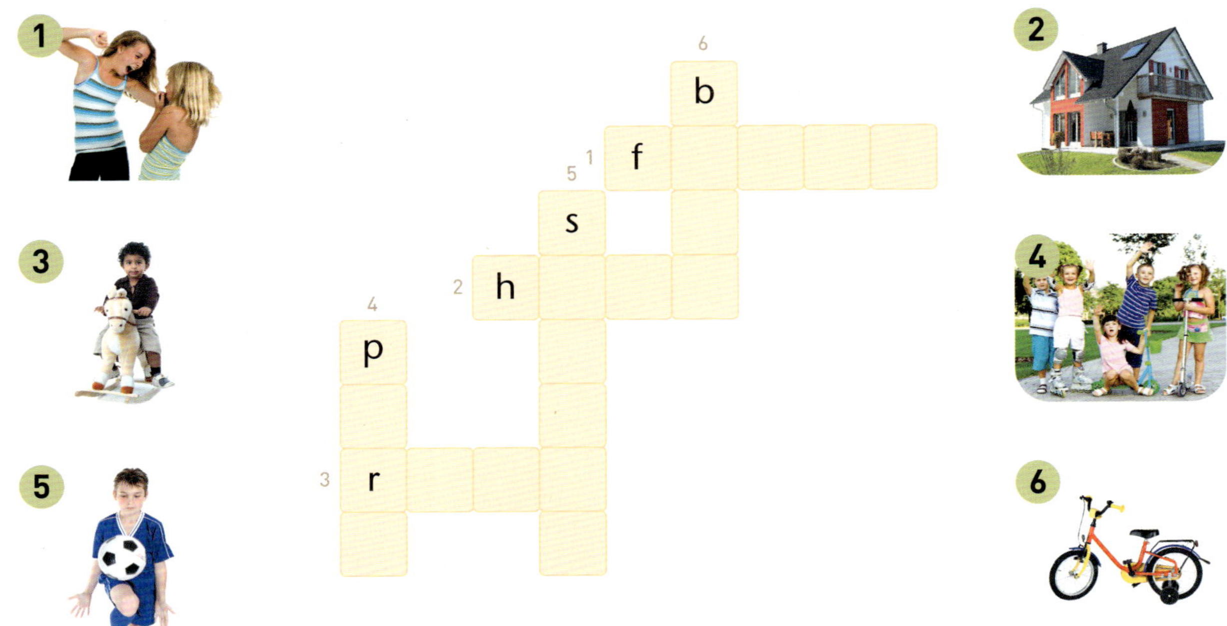

Grammar Practice Look and write.

1. We ride bikes. (always)

➡ _______________________________

2. We go to the park. (usually)

➡ _______________________________

3. We fight. (sometimes)

➡ _______________________________

1. best / Jacob and I / are / friends / .

2. sometimes / We / play / soccer / .

3. always / We / "I'm sorry." / say,

Dictation Listen and fill in the blanks. 

Jacob and I are ________________ friends.

We never stay home.

We always ________________ bikes.

We usually go to the ________________ .

We sometimes play tag.

We sometimes jump rope.

We sometimes play soccer.

We sometimes ________________ , too.

But we always say, "I'm sorry."

01 At a Flower Garden

Word Review Choose and complete.

1. 

yell⬜w

2. 

flo⬜er

3. 

li⬜y

| i | w | l | s | c | o |

4. 

⬜unflower

5. 

inse⬜t

6. 

wh⬜te

Grammar Practice Read and circle.

1. 

Q: What do you see?

A: I see one yellow (flower / flowers).

2. 

Q: What do you see?

A: I see three white (flower / flowers).

3. 

Q: What do you see?

A: I see one (insect / insects).

1. do / What / see / you / ?

2. see / I / flower / yellow / one / .

3. a sunflower / It / is / .

Dictation Listen and fill in the blanks. 

What do you see?

I see one ________________ flower.

It is a sunflower.

What do you see?

I see ________________ white flowers.

They are lilies.

________________ do you see?

Oh! I see one ________________ .

It is a honeybee. Bzzz.

02 What Plants Need

Word Review Circle and match.

1. 

2. 

3. 

food sunlight air plant water grow

4. 

5. 

6. 

Grammar Practice Read and circle.

1.  Jane (need / needs) water.

2.  Plants (need / don't need) air.

3.  Plants don't (need / needs) meat and vegetables.

1. needs / water / Jane / .

2. sunlight / Plants / need / .

3. meat and vegetables / don't / Plants / need / .

Dictation Listen and fill in the blanks. 

Jane needs _________________ .

Plants need water, too.

Jane needs _________________ .

Plants need air, too.

Jane _______________ food.

Plants need food, too.

But plants don't need _______________ and vegetables.

Plants need sunlight.

With water, air, and sunlight, plants _________________ .

UNIT 7 01

Goldfish Facts

Word Review Find and circle.

1
sleep

3
eat

5
fish

o	s	h	a	r	k	r	j	m
d	f	i	s	h	g	j	b	u
q	k	l	l	y	p	o	o	l
e	v	h	e	u	j	t	a	e
v	e	g	e	t	a	b	l	e
c	w	y	p	l	i	a	t	n

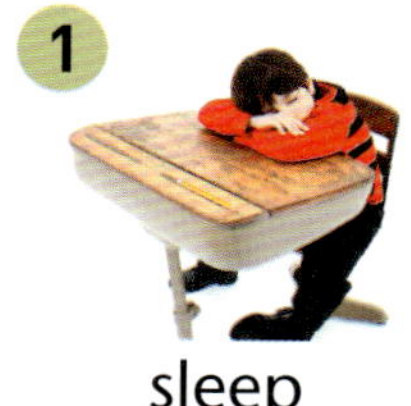

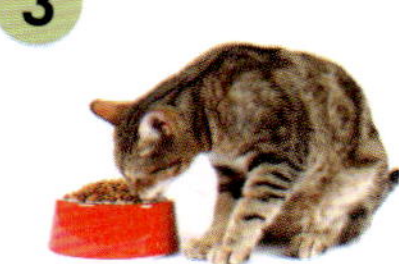

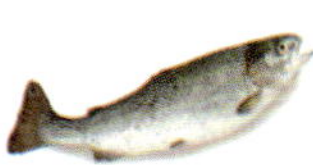

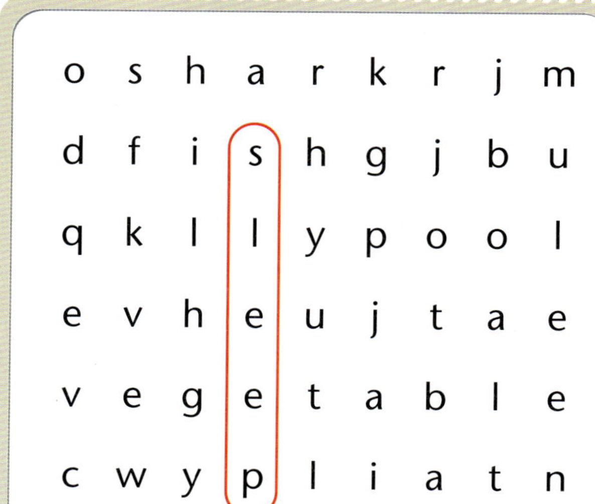

2
pool

4
shark

6
vegetable

Grammar Practice Read and circle.

1.

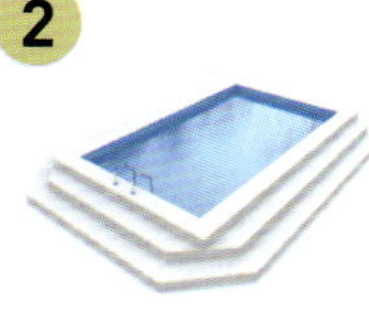

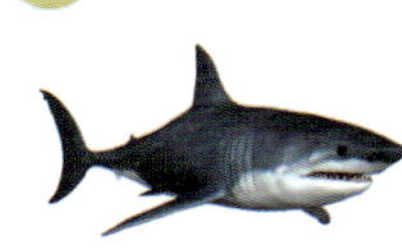

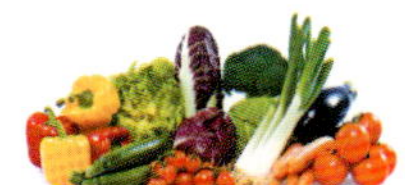

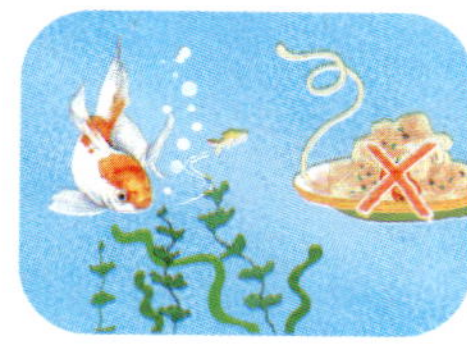

Goldfish eat vegetables.

They (eat / don't eat) spaghetti.

2.

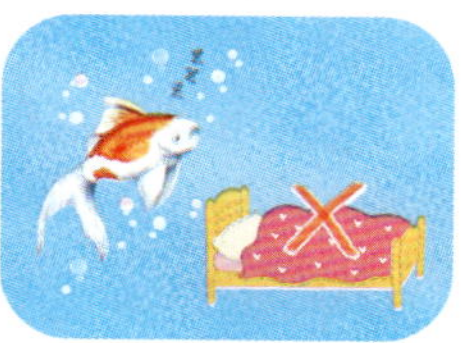

Goldfish sleep.

They (sleep / don't sleep) in beds.

3.

Goldfish (live / don't live) in water.

They don't live in pools.

Writing Practice **Unscramble and write.**

1. live / Goldfish / in / water / .

2. together / play / Goldfish / .

3. don't play / They / sharks / with / .

Dictation **Listen and fill in the blanks.** 

Do you know about _________________ ?

Goldfish eat fish and vegetables.

But they don't _______________ spaghetti.

Goldfish sleep.

But they don't sleep in beds.

Goldfish _________________ in water.

But they don't live in pools.

Goldfish play _________________ .

But they don't play with sharks.

What a Funny Bird!

Word Review Do the crossword.

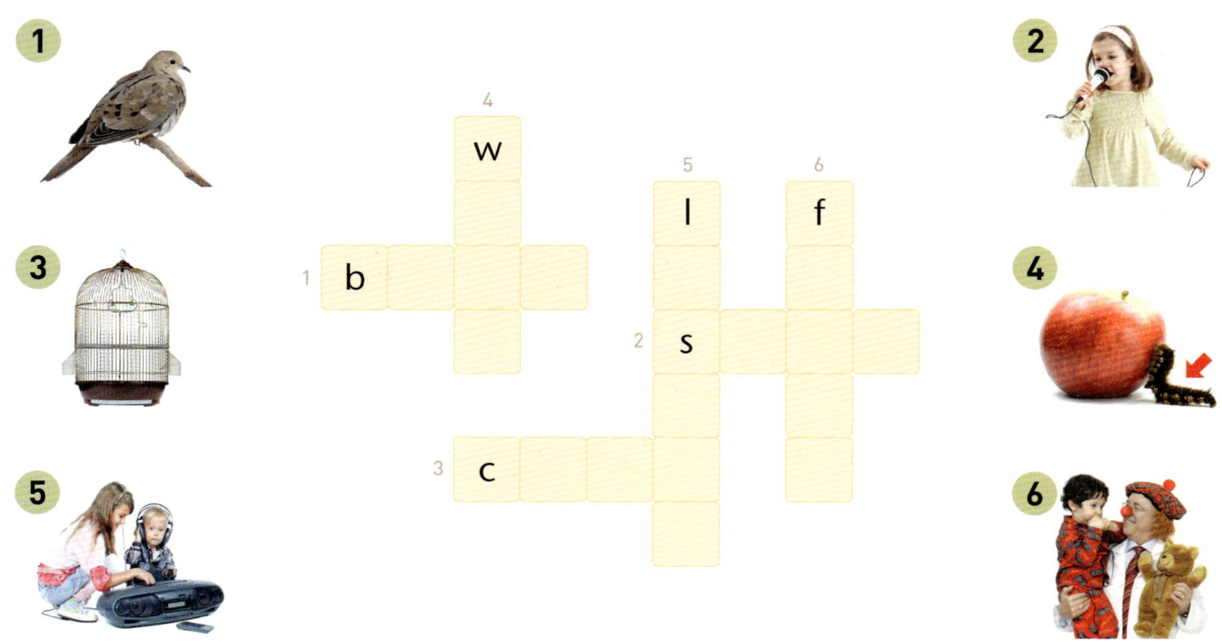

Grammar Practice Read and circle.

1. Coco (lives / doesn't live) in a cage.

2. Coco (listens / doesn't listen) to jazz.

3. Coco (eats / doesn't eat) worms.

1. a dog house / lives / She / in / .

2. bird / do / things / Coco / doesn't / .

3. my / I / bird / love / funny / !

Dictation Listen and fill in the blanks. 

My bird, Coco, is ________________ .

She doesn't live in a ________________ .

She lives in a dog house.

She doesn't ________________ songs.

She listens to jazz.

She doesn't eat ________________ .

She eats garlic bread.

Coco doesn't do bird things.

But I love my funny bird!

01 What a Bad Day!

Word Review Choose and complete.

1. 

h☐de

2. 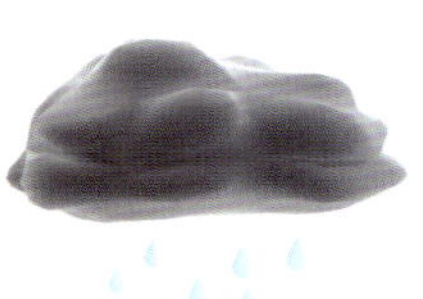

r☐in

3. 

☐air

| a | h | i | o | c | w |

4. 

fa☐e

5. 

☐ind

6. 

cl☐ud

Grammar Practice Look, choose and write.

1. 

Q: _____________ the weather today?

A: It's rainy.

2. 

Q: How's the weather today?

A: _____________ windy.

3. 

Q: How's the weather?

A: It's ___________.

How's
What's
It's
cloud
cloudy

1. blowing / The wind / my hair / is / .

2. It / is / today / a bad / day / .

3. tomorrow / the weather / How's / ?

Dictation Listen and fill in the blanks. 

It is windy today.

The wind is blowing my _______________ .

It is cloudy today.

The clouds are _______________ the sun.

It is rainy today.

The rain is falling on my _______________ .

It is a bad day today.

How's the _______________ tomorrow?

Safe in the Sun

Word Review Circle and match.

1. 

2. 

3. 

4. 

5. 

6. 

Grammar Practice Read and choose.

1. 
Q: (Do / Did) you wear sunscreen in the summer?
A: Yes, I do.

2. 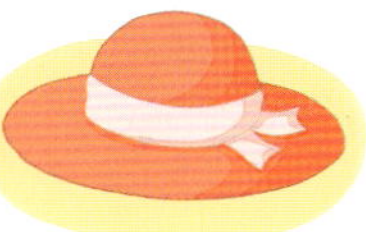
Q: Do you (wear / wearing) a hat in the summer?
A: Yes, I do.

3. 
Q: Do you wear sunglasses in the summer?
A: Yes, (I do / do I).

Writing Practice Unscramble and write.

1. a hat / Do / wear / you / ?

2. you / drink / Do / water / ?

3. in / safe / the sun / Stay / .

Dictation Listen and fill in the blanks. 

Do you wear sunscreen?

Do you wear a ________________?

Do you wear sunglasses?

Do you drink water?

Do you ________________ and rest?

Let's answer, "Yes, I do!"

And stay ________________ in the sun.

01 My Senses

Word Review Find and circle.

1 
taste

3 
nose

5 
smell

x	d	s	u	t	m	j	s
j	l	m	h	a	o	e	e
o	k	e	p	s	u	s	a
m	a	l	p	t	t	r	r
r	o	l	o	e	h	d	z
x	q	d	n	o	s	e	p

2 
ear

4 
hear

6 
mouth

Grammar Practice Read and circle.

1.  My ears (can / can't) hear.

2.  My nose (can / can't) see.

3.  My eyes (can / can't) taste.

Writing Practice Unscramble and write.

1. ears / hear / can / My / .

2. taste / mouth / My / can / .

3. it / But / see / can't / .

Dictation Listen and fill in the blanks. 

My ears can _________________ .

But they can't smell.

My _______________ can smell.

But it can't see.

My _______________ can see.

But they can't taste.

My _______________ can taste.

But it can't hear!

Clean Hands, Healthy Hands

Word Review Do the crossword.

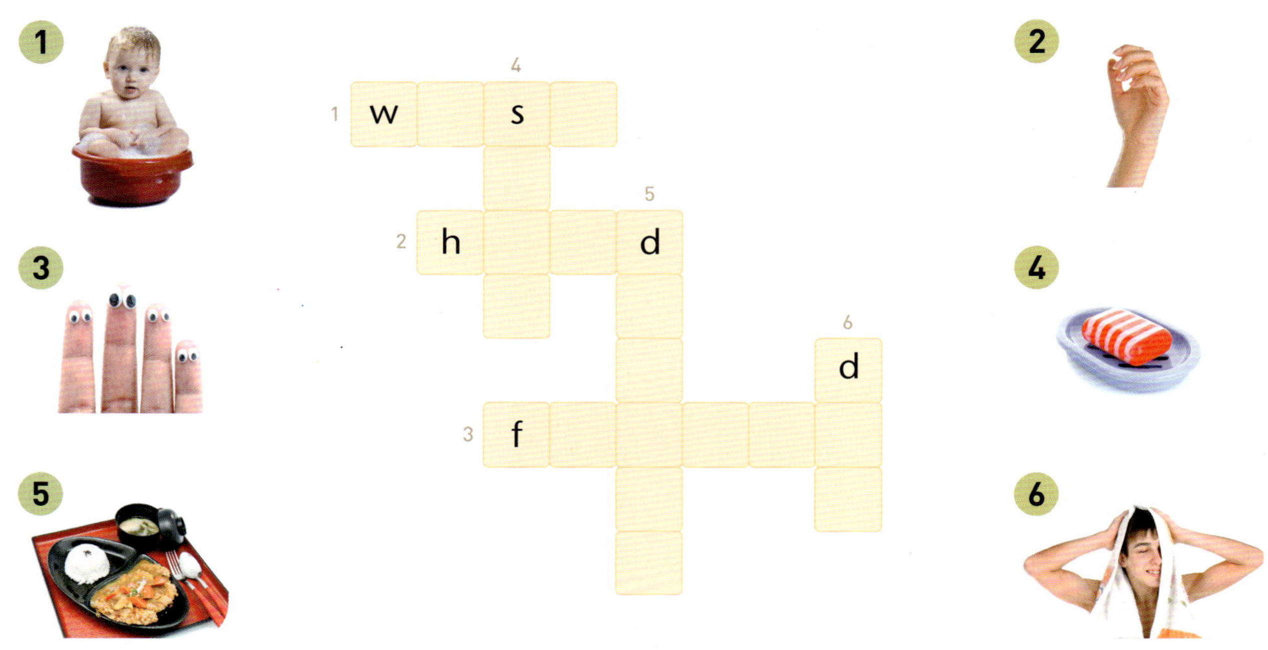

Grammar Practice Read and match.

1. Wet your hands •   • your hands.

2. Put some soap •   • with water.

3. Rinse and dry •   • on your hands.

1. for / It's / dinner / time / .

2. need to / You / wash / your hands / .

3. between / Wash / your / fingers / .

Dictation Listen and fill in the blanks. 

It's time for dinner.

You need to wash your hands.

First, _______________ your hands with water.

Next, put some soap on your _______________.

Then, rub your hands together.

Wash between your fingers, too!

Finally, _______________ and dry your hands.

Now, they are _______________.

Let's eat!

At the Zoo

Word Review Choose and complete.

1. ti☐ed

2. lio☐

3. bo☐t

4. co☐d

5. dol☐hin

6. s☐ared

Grammar Practice Read and circle.

1.

Q: Are the (penguin / penguins) cold?

A: No, they aren't.

2.

Q: (Is / Are) the lion scared?

A: No, it isn't.

3.

Q: Are the dolphins tired?

A: No, they (isn't / aren't).

Writing Practice Unscramble and write.

1. have / The penguins / coats / don't / .

2. doesn't / The lion / have / a flashlight / .

3. tired / they / Are / ?

Dictation Listen and fill in the blanks. 

The penguins don't have _________________.

Are they cold?

No, they aren't.

The lion doesn't have a flashlight.

Is it _______________?

No, it isn't.

The dolphins don't have _______________.

Are they _______________?

No, they aren't. But I am!

02 Sick Day

Word Review Circle and match.

1. 
2. 
3. 

m i l k b r i n g r e a d s i c k s o u p f e e l

4. 
5. 
6. 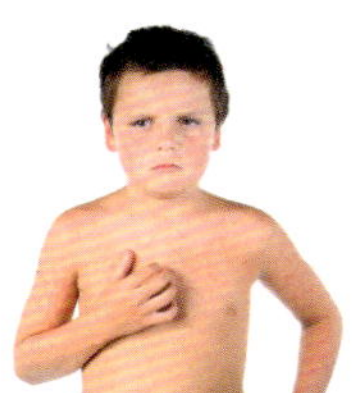

Grammar Practice Read and write.

1. 
My mom is brining soup.
But I'm ________________.
(not eat)

2. 
My mom is brining milk
But I'm ________________.
(not drink)

3. 
My mom is brining books.
But I'm ________________.
(not read)

Writing Practice Unscramble and write.

1. sick / today / I / am feeling / .

____

____

____

2. am staying / I / in bed / .

____

____

____

3. reading / am not / I / .

____

____

____

Dictation Listen and fill in the blanks. 

I am feeling ________________ today.

I am ________________ in bed.

My mom is bringing soup.

But I'm not eating.

My mom is ________________ milk.

But I'm not drinking.

My mom is bringing books.

But I'm not reading.

I am just ________________ and sleeping.

Reading Start is a three-leveled reading series designed for low beginner students to strengthen the foundation of reading skills. Accompanied by fascinating visuals, this series equips students with a wide vocabulary while developing reading skills. Theme-based stories guide students to use their imagination as they explore various fiction stories and nonfiction articles. The follow-on activities are designed to strengthen their speaking and listening skills. This series is full of all the necessary tools students need to improve their overall English ability.

Key Features:

★ Theme-based topics with interesting stories
★ Captivating images to stimulate imaginations
★ Variation in vocabulary expansion activities
★ Further speaking and listening activities
★ Full engagement in reading with lively animated audio CD

Components

★ Student Book / Workbook / Audio CD
★ MP3 Files / Answer Keys
   Download resources at **www.wcbooks.co.kr**

Reading Start Series